Praise for
Out of a Far Country

"Christopher Yuan and Angela Yuan have told the story of their miraculous journey from broken lives, relationships, and dreams to a place of hope and healing. *Out of a Far Country* brings home the living truth that in the midst of a broken and hurting world, God is at work to redeem, renew, and reconcile his beloved. I'm particularly happy to endorse this book because Christopher, like myself, was broken in prison and redeemed by Christ."

> —CHUCK COLSON, founder of Prison Fellowship and the Chuck
> Colson Center for Christian Worldview

"*Out of a Far Country* reads like a modern rendition of the prodigal son parable, only it is more gripping. The journey taken by Christopher Yuan is rarely documented. Be prepared, for the raw emotions of both mother and son authentically mark every page. The spiritual lessons to be gained from this book are many. May it gain a vast audience!"

> —J. PAUL NYQUIST, PhD, president of Moody Bible Institute

"This is a moving account of how an Asian mother's fragile love turns into a prayerful, patient, and tenacious force of forgiveness. It is also a gripping narrative of a son's search for belonging and meaning. *Out of a Far Country* breeds hope in every despairing heart."

> —LISA ESPINELI CHINN, director of International Student
> Ministries for InterVarsity/USA

"The Good Shepherd knows his sheep and calls them by name. Christopher Yuan, trapped in a life of drugs and sexual addiction, heard that call and rose to follow Jesus. His and his mother's account of that rising is a profound story of redemption that all of us in this broken generation need to hear."

> —DUANE LITFIN, president emeritus of Wheaton College in Illinois

"Relevant, courageous, fascinating, and much more. I have known the Yuans for many years, and their walk is in line with their talk. This important and needed story goes against the wind, but it is one hundred percent in the right direction."

—Dr. George Verwer, founder and former international director of Operation Mobilisation

"*Out of a Far Country* is a true-life parable of saving grace for a prodigal mother and a wayward son who needed God's forgiveness. Their story will warm the heart and lift the spirit of every parent who prays for a wandering child and every believer who needs to be reminded why the gospel is good news."

—Dr. Philip G. Ryken, president of Wheaton College in Illinois

"At one point, Angela and Christopher were living worlds apart. I have heard their story countless times, and it never grows old. I know you will be amazed by the God who did the impossible to bring this mother and son back together."

—Alan Chambers, president of Exodus International

"This is the story of God's persistent chase of a wayward son through the prayers and love of a determined mother. But even more, it is a testimony to the fact that loving God is a far more satisfying pursuit than following our own desires. I am thankful that Christopher and Angela are willing to be so transparent about their journey. Christopher's desire to follow Christ regardless of the struggle stands as a model for all who desire to love God with all their heart."

—Dr. Joseph M. Stowell, president of Cornerstone University in Grand Rapids, Michigan

"God snatched Christopher Yuan from a desperately empty life and offered him the hope of Jesus Christ. This is a story of God's redemption, love, and mercy in the midst of overwhelming sin and a heart that was far from God. Get two copies of this book—you will want to give one to a friend who needs Jesus."

—Dr. James MacDonald, senior pastor of Harvest Bible Chapel in Rolling Meadows, Illinois

OUT OF A FAR COUNTRY

A gay **son's** journey to God.
A broken **mother's** search for hope.

OUT OF A FAR COUNTRY

Christopher Yuan
& Angela Yuan

WATERBROOK
PRESS

Out of a Far Country
Published by WaterBrook Press
12265 Oracle Boulevard, Suite 200
Colorado Springs, Colorado 80921

The story that is told in this book is entirely true. In an effort to safeguard the privacy of individuals whose lives have touched the lives of the authors, some of the names of the people mentioned in this book have been changed.

ISBN 978-0-307-72935-4
ISBN 978-0-307-72936-1 (electronic)

Cover design by Kelly L. Howard; photography by JHB Studio/Images.com

Library of Congress Cataloging-in-Publication Data
Yuan, Christopher.
   Out of a far country : a gay son's journey to God : a broken mother's search for hope / Christopher Yuan and Angela Yuan. — 1st ed.
      p. cm.
   Includes bibliographical references.
   ISBN 978-0-307-72935-4 — ISBN 978-0-307-72936-1 (editorial)
   1. Yuan, Christopher. 2. Yuan, Angela. 3. Christian gay men—United States—Biography. 4. Drug dealers—United States—Biography. 5. Chinese Americans—Biography. 6. Mothers and sons. 7. Gay men—Family relationships. I. Yuan, Angela. II. Title.
   HQ75.8.Y83A3 2011
   261.8'357662092—dc22
   [B]

                                                2010053733

Printed in the United States of America
2011

10 9 8 7 6 5

Special Sales
Most WaterBrook Multnomah books are available at special quantity discounts when purchased in bulk by corporations, organizations, and special-interest groups. Custom imprinting or excerpting can also be done to fit special needs. For information, please e-mail SpecialMarkets@WaterBrookMultnomah.com or call 1-800-603-7051.

— — —

For Leon, husband and father:
Thank you for being willing to change,
not giving up on us, and continuing to pursue Christ.

CONTENTS

FOREWORD

Inspiring books have been written about Jesus's parable of the prodigal son, the younger of two brothers who left his family to pursue a different way of living. We know only a few details about the choices made by the biblical prodigal, and the outcomes of his choices. If we knew more about the things that took place in the far country, I imagine Jesus's story recorded in the gospel of Luke would stop us in our tracks. What we do know is that the younger brother led a life of his own choosing, then came back home a humbled, defeated person. The glory of the story is that he was welcomed by his loving, waiting father.

The story that is told in this book contains similar elements, but it features two prodigals, a younger son and his mother. The son left home to go to graduate school, and after a few years he began living in a way that went against his parents' values. His mother, driven by love but also battered by shame and distraught over a lifeless marriage, came to the end of herself (see Luke 15:17, KJV). As hard as this was, it proved to be a turning point for both mother and son.

Out of a Far Country speaks directly to anyone who has wandered for any length of time. It's a blindingly true story that will resonate with prodigal sons and daughters, and with the parents of prodigals. This story is sometimes heartbreaking, and it's often raw in its honesty. The battle that is waged over a person's soul is lengthy and hard fought, and the outcome is not known until after wounds have been suffered.

But the end of the story for a humbled, repentant prodigal—whether son, daughter, or parent—is one of God's open arms, his love and sacrifice, and his grace to save us. That story never loses its power.

This book tells a story that will inspire you, and it's one you can learn from. It will guide you to seek God and his help, even in times when your life gives no indication that there is any hope left. Christopher Yuan and

Angela Yuan are two prodigals who chose finally to come back to their Father. Their story will give you hope—or restore your hope if you have lost it.

> But when he was yet a great way off, his father saw him, and had compassion, and ran, and fell on his neck, and kissed him. (Luke 15:20, kjv)

—Kay Warren
Cofounder of Saddleback Church, Lake Forest, California
Founder of the HIV/AIDS Initiative, Saddleback Church

ACKNOWLEDGMENTS

First, thanks to Bucky Rosenbaum, our wonderful agent. You saw potential in this story and believed in it from the beginning. Thanks for leading us on this exciting journey.

Chris Fabry, you helped us get our thoughts organized. Kate Etue, you are a lifesaver. Without you we could not have completed the book, and your commitment and talent show through in the final version.

Julie, Jessica, Anna, Eric, Vivian, Bruce, Stephanie, Christine, Betty, Winnie, Steven, Tiffanie, and Jenny, you diligently transcribed interview transcripts in a time crunch. Thank you for your speed and accuracy! Julie Chen, your talents really helped us when we were in a time crunch. Thanks, Sarah Lin, for selflessly helping us all the way from Taiwan.

We are ever grateful to our church families and Bible Study Fellowship partners. You prayed alongside us and tied yellow ribbons to welcome this prodigal son home. We are so grateful for Moody Bible Institute and Wheaton College for giving Christopher a second chance and for your continued enthusiastic support.

FROM ANGELA

Muriel Milem, you are my mentor, prayer warrior, encourager, and friend. Your help editing the outline of this book and our proposal was invaluable. Sandy Long, during my difficult years of waiting, you cried with me, laughed with me, and went above and beyond to pull me through. Mabel Jung, you are closer to me than a sister. You've stuck with me through the ups and downs for fifty-five years. Hover and Joanne, you are so willing to be available and have such servant hearts.

From Christopher

Joe Hendrickson, you are a great brother in Christ who over the years has prayed with me and held me accountable. Thanks for running the race with me. Karen Swanson and Brenda Ratcliff, you encouraged me to write this book and are two of my biggest cheerleaders! Rosalie de Roset and Karyn Hecht, thanks for taking time to proofread early writing samples. George Verwer, you are like a mentor to me with your numerous and timely calls from around the globe. Your concern for my health and my spiritual walk blesses me immensely.

— — —

And much appreciation to Ron Lee and the team at WaterBrook Multnomah for walking alongside us throughout this exciting journey and making this deeply emotional experience of putting our life stories on paper a pleasant one!

Lastly, we want to thank our Lord, Jesus Christ. He is the true Author of this story.

> Oh, the depth of the riches of the wisdom and knowledge of God!
>> How unsearchable his judgments,
>> and his paths beyond tracing out!
> "Who has known the mind of the Lord?
>> Or who has been his counselor?"
> "Who has ever given to God,
>> that God should repay him?"
> For from him and through him and to him are all things.
>> To him be the glory forever! Amen.
>> (Romans 11:33–36)

One doesn't ask of one who suffers: what is
your country and what is your religion? One
merely says, You suffer, this is enough for me.
You belong to me, and I shall help you.

—Louis Pasteur

God, you did everything you promised,
    and I'm thanking you with all my heart.
You pulled me from the brink of death,
    my feet from the cliff-edge of doom.
Now I stroll at leisure with God
    in the sunlit fields of life.

—Psalm 56:12–13 (msg)

One

The End of My World

Angela: May 15, 1993

It was May in Chicago. The warmth of spring was starting to wrap its arms around the city we had called home for twenty-four years. But that night we sat in silence, picking at our stir-fry with forks as cold and hard as our hearts.

Dinner was miserable, and it had nothing to do with the food.

You'd think that after so many years of living with my disconnected but often argumentative husband, Leon, I'd be used to misery. But this night was unusually dismal.

Our younger son, Christopher, was home for a visit. He had just finished his junior year of dental school in Louisville, Kentucky, after transferring from Loyola University School of Dentistry in Chicago the previous fall. Leon, a dentist himself, was glad that Christopher was following in his footsteps. It was expected that in a year father and son would be working together in our new dental office.

Of course, I too had been looking forward to Christopher's visit. Like any good Chinese mother, I doted on our two sons, but Christopher and I had always been especially close. Normally his being at home would keep the tension in our home from boiling over. But Christopher's presence at the dinner table tonight only elevated our family's permanent state of emotional strain.

— — —

A few days before Christopher had come home, Leon was checking the insulation in the crawlspace just off Christopher's bedroom. On his way out of the crawlspace, the beam from his flashlight landed on something tucked away on top of the small access opening. He discovered an un-labeled VHS tape in a worn cardboard case, which he brought down-stairs to show me.

As soon as I saw the dusty videocassette, I froze. I knew what it was, but everything inside me hoped it wasn't. The truth was, for six years I had feared that Christopher's problem had never really gone away.

I couldn't bring myself to watch what was on the tape, so I asked Leon to do it. He took it from my hand and went into the living room to play it. Finally, he walked back into the kitchen, dropped the tape on the counter, and said, "Yes, it's that."

That. He couldn't even say the word. It was gay pornography.

I immediately thought back to when Christopher was sixteen years old and I found out from his brother that he had had a sexual relationship with a thirty-year-old man. Christopher had contacted the man, who then invited him over. Sure, Christopher may have sought the man out, but no matter how you look at it, this man had used and soiled my son.

Words cannot express what I felt at that time. Sadness and deep an-guish overwhelmed me. But I was also furious at the man who took ad-vantage of my son. Christopher was robbed of the chance to be a normal teenager, and what's worse, I couldn't tell anyone about it. I wanted to see this man brought to justice, but that meant making a horrific private matter a public one. And I would not allow Christopher to go through that humiliation. We decided not to press charges, choosing instead to keep the heartache and shame a secret.

Added to the terrible disgrace was constant anxiety. During Christo-pher's teenage years, my days were filled with fear. I worried about what people would say if they found out. I worried about how much Christopher was scarred, and whether his future would be affected by this incident. I especially worried about whether he would become...gay.

Even though this was a very private matter, I knew we should do something to find help. That same day, I had been flipping through material from a dental-office management company. This company helped us better manage our practice in order to increase the dental-office income. In this literature, I read about a counseling program offered by the parent organization. It promised resources for dealing with life's problems, and the sponsoring organization was the Church of Scientology. I had never heard of Scientology. I was skeptical, but desperate. I would do anything to fix my son.

So Christopher and I traveled from Chicago to the Scientology Mission of San Francisco, where we enrolled in a program that required us to be there mornings and afternoons for two months. Certainly, their techniques were a little bizarre—sitting in a sauna for hours or holding metal cans during counseling (or "auditing") sessions. But I was determined to beat this—for Christopher's sake. Failure was not an option that I was willing to consider.

After two months and more than fifteen thousand dollars, we finished the purification program. More important, Christopher assured me that he was over that phase and ready to move on with life. I thought we had it all taken care of.

— — —

But on a beautiful afternoon in May 1993, I sat picking at my stir-fry. I was waiting for the right moment to say something, but I had no idea what to say. I glanced to my right at Leon, trying to read his dark eyes. Was he going to confront Christopher as I wished, or wasn't he? He briefly looked at me, then resumed his eating, oblivious to my agony. Leon wasn't going to say anything, and as always his indifference drove me crazy. Once again, we weren't on the same page. Once again, he had no idea how I felt.

Vei-Chi Chiang

Our wedding took place at Notre Dame Church in Central Park, Manhattan, on September 11, 1965. My father is on the far right. I had no idea how difficult life would become after this day.

I could tell that Christopher knew I was upset. Our relationship had been strained in recent months. He'd been acting rudely to me—more like a resentful teenager than a twenty-two-year-old doctoral student. And this night only added to the tension. He kept looking at his watch and seemed to be contemplating a quick exit.

Leon still hadn't said anything, and Christopher was about to leave the table. I needed an answer from my son, and I knew I had to speak up. If homosexuality was still a problem for Christopher, then we needed to take action.

"Christopher, Dad found a videotape in your crawlspace." My voice was shaking—with fear, with despair? I never shied away from confrontation, but this was different.

Christopher looked at me with a blank face. No emotion, no guilt, not even surprise.

"Dad watched it," I whispered. I swallowed hard, wishing this were a nightmare and I would wake up and everything would be okay. I wished my son would tell me what I wanted to hear—even if it wasn't true. Besides, how could Christopher still be that? After all I had done for him.

But he just kept giving me that empty look.

"Christopher"—I forced the words out—"are you...are you still...?"

The question hung there, but only for a moment. Christopher sat up straight, looked me in the eyes, and with a voice full of resolve said, "Yes, I am. I am gay."

He spoke confidently, without disgrace or apology. I couldn't believe my ears. There was such boldness, as if he were proud of it. But shame swept over me. This couldn't be true. Not my son, not my Christopher. At that moment, I wished the house would fall down on us and put an end to this mess.

I'd always had our lives all figured out. Christopher and his brother would grow up and accomplish important things in the world. They were both studying to be dentists. They would return home when they earned their degrees, join their father's practice, and ultimately inherit the family business. Leon and I were just then completing a brand-new, state-of-the-art dental office. I would be at the helm, managing the office and making sure everything ran like a well-oiled machine. It would give me the life I longed for—spending time with my family and keeping us all together.

But now this.

I looked from my son to my husband and back again. I was as disappointed with Leon as I had ever been. Even though our marriage was totally lifeless, at least he should be concerned about his own son. So today, with Christopher announcing he was gay, why wasn't Leon stepping in to do something? Why didn't he say anything? Why wasn't he outraged? Why wasn't he telling Christopher that he was not, could not be...gay?

It was obvious to me that Christopher was not thinking clearly. Didn't he know that he couldn't choose both—to be a dentist and to live like that? If people knew, Leon would lose his patients. If people knew, no staff would work with us. If people knew, they would be afraid of getting AIDS. Christopher needed to come to his senses and be reminded that this family practice was everything. It had been our one dream—everything we had worked toward—for almost twenty years.

"Christopher," I blurted out his name in frustration. "You must choose. You must choose the family or choose homosexuality." This ultimatum would wake him up. He would have to choose his family and not throw away this bright future in our new office.

My son looked at me and said, "It's not something I can choose. I was born this way... I am gay." He took a deep breath and looked away. His neck tightened and his jaw clenched as he looked back at me with an expression I had never seen before. "If you can't accept me, then I have no other choice but to leave."

He backed away from the table and uttered one last cutting remark. "I expected you'd react like this. But that's okay. I have a family. A real family of friends back in Louisville who accept me"—his voice cracked—"for exactly who I am."

He went to his room. In a few minutes he came back through the house with his bags and walked out the door. It was as if he had planned this all along. There was no room for discussion, no time for negotiation. That was it. This was the end.

My knees gave way, and I fell to the floor. I felt as if my blood drained out of my body. My arms, my hands, my legs were cold as ice. The weight of shock and disbelief weighed so heavily on my chest that I had to strain just to breathe. This couldn't be happening.

I began gasping for air. I was choking on my tears, knowing without question that I was a total failure. My marriage had been a failure for years, and now my parenting was a failure. My husband refused to stand by me. My older son had rebelled. And now Christopher, the one I thought would never do this to me, had rejected me.

I wanted to make Christopher stay, but I was out of options. And

Leon still hadn't said anything. He didn't yell at Christopher or argue with him. Neither did he put his arm around me or hold my hand. He just walked away, leaving me lying on the floor alone, gasping between sobs.

A thought entered my mind, a memory of something Leon's mother had told him. My mother-in-law had said a wife uses three tricks when she doesn't get her way. First, she cries; second, she throws a temper tantrum; third, she threatens to hang herself. On that day, I was not playing any tricks. I was certain that I had nothing left to live for.

Two

Out of the Closet

Christopher: May 15, 1993

I saw my mother fall to the floor as I closed the door to leave. Just more Chinese-mother guilt-trip drama, I figured. I had seen too much of it over the years to be manipulated by it again. Besides, I wasn't Chinese. I was American, born and raised in Chicago.

My gay friends in Louisville had told me what to expect when I came out to my parents—the screaming, the crying, the "after all I've done for you" routine. My mother didn't disappoint, that's for sure. And my father was true to form as well. He wasn't even engaged enough to be for me or against me.

After almost a year of being active in Louisville's gay community, I was ready to come out to my parents. I'd halfway planned to do it when I came home for Mother's Day a week earlier, but I wasn't sure how to bring it up. So at the dinner table, it was actually a relief when my mother confronted me. Now I was finally all the way out of the closet. In the gay community, coming out to your parents is a rite of passage. It's taking the final step in fully embracing your homosexuality. And having completed that step, I had climbed one rung higher on the social ladder.

After hearing my friends' horror stories, I was expecting to get kicked out of my parents' house—and that's exactly what happened. When my mother asked me to choose between homosexuality and the family, it meant that I couldn't be true to myself *and* be accepted by my parents. And among my friends, I'd gotten used to being accepted. Mom was effectively kicking me out.

That hurt. But the hurt was overshadowed by the relief I felt. I could finally write my parents off. I didn't have to care about them anymore, because they obviously didn't care about me. They weren't my real family. Real family would have accepted me for who I was. My gay friends in Louisville were now my real family.

The farther south I drove from Chicago, the freer I felt. In fact, I had never felt so free. No more having to hide. No more making up stories. No more family obligations. No more putting up with the nightly phone calls from home just to "check in."

My whole life I had been entangled in my mother's apron strings. She controlled every aspect of my life—or tried to. When I went away to college, she called every night to check on me. When I went away to boot camp with the Marine Corps, she demanded that I write home all the time. Even when I was in graduate school, she refused to let me live my own life. But things would be different now. She had kicked me out of the family, and all the meddling would come to an end.

- - -

Midway through my first year at the University of Louisville, I came out of the closet to my friends and classmates. It was a freeing experience, and I'd never felt happier. Finally I could stop pretending, and I could be honest with friends who thought I was straight.

One day my good friend and workout partner, Gary, told me, "Rumors are going around the school that you're gay. I've been defending you, telling people it's not true, telling them that you've had several girlfriends." He lowered his voice and his face became serious. "It's not true, is it?"

He was shocked when I told him it was. He'd meant well when he told others that I was straight. He really thought he was defending me

Olan Mills Inc.

Mom wanted me to write home all the time while away at Marine Corps boot camp. I was a reservist when this photo was taken in 1989.

from vicious rumors. But the rumors were true. While I wasn't effeminate or flamboyant, I was gay.

As more people became aware of my real life, I felt more comfortable with my homosexuality. I no longer tried to hide it. If people weren't okay with it, I didn't care. For the first time, I felt I was being completely honest. Living any other way would be a lie.

It just so happened that two gay clubs in the city, the Connection and the Annex, were only five blocks from the dental school. I'd been to a few gay bars in Chicago, clubs that were more a place to cruise or hook up than a place to belong. But most of the men I met in the Louisville bars seemed…normal. They were professionals—bankers, lawyers, executives, dental students. Men like me. I went from thinking, *There's something wrong with me,* to, *This is who I am.* These people were my friends. This was where I belonged.

When I was growing up, kids picked on me for being Chinese, playing the piano, loving the arts, and showing my feelings more than most boys did. I was horrible at sports, and I always felt like an outcast. But when I stepped into the gay community, I was introduced to a world of outcasts who had come together and become family. They stood up for one another, supported one another. They laughed with me, cried with me, and accepted me for who I was—gay.

With my newfound confidence, I became popular in the gay club scene. Never one to be much of a drinker, I started bartending for fun— and was quite successful at it. My outgoing personality and good physique made a difference in that setting, where bartenders often worked shirtless to show off their bodies. I made good tips—especially when I climbed on the bar and danced. After a childhood of being rejected by my peers, it felt great to be so readily accepted.

Telling my parents was the final hurdle in coming out. I knew they would be unwilling to let go of their set ways. It would have been awkward if my mother had said, "You're gay? Great! Why don't I come down to Louisville and you can introduce me to some of your gay friends?" Nevertheless, their rejection showed me how closed minded they were. At the same time, I fully expected them not to understand me. Their reaction fit in with the other coming-out war stories I'd heard. There was a pretty standard script for gay folks, and the big blowup with the parents was the climactic scene that marked the end of act one and the beginning of act two.

— — —

Never before had I so looked forward to getting back to Louisville. Driving away from Chicago on Interstate 65 didn't feel like leaving home; I felt like I was going home. And there was someone special I was going back to.

A couple of weeks earlier, I had started a new relationship. Grant was older than I was—well into his thirties—good looking, well built, successful, and generous. He was a lawyer, involved in Kentucky state politics, and he lived in a beautiful guest house on a big estate. Shortly before my trip to Chicago, Grant had invited me to move out of the fraternity house on the university campus where I'd been staying and move in with him. Now I was anxious to get back to him and our new home together.

I'd had a few boyfriends before Grant, but he was different—mature, professional, and stable. Stable, that's what I wanted in a relationship. I wanted to settle down, and my heart raced just thinking about moving into his house. It was the first time that I'd felt sure that another man really cared about me—enough to invite me into his home. I was finally in a relationship that had a future.

As I drove back to Kentucky, I was sure that Grant's acceptance would buffer the pain of my parents' rejection. I was glad that finally there were no more barriers between me and my happiness with Grant.

At last I pulled into the long, tree-lined driveway leading to Grant's house. It was a little after midnight, but I knew he was a night owl and would still be up. I parked in front and bounded up the steps to the front door. I was supposed to be in Chicago another day and was excited to surprise Grant with my early return. I let myself into the house. "Hey, Grant! I'm back!" I called into the darkness.

When I saw his face, I knew something was wrong. He didn't run to embrace me. He didn't break into a grin. He just stood there looking at me, not bothering to interrupt the awkward silence. Then he said, "Hey...you're back already. I wasn't expecting you so soon."

"Yeah, I hoped I'd surprise you. My parents—"

"Listen, we need to talk… Um, maybe it would be best if we…um… cooled it for a bit."

"What do you mean?"

"Maybe you should stay at the frat house tonight."

I was crushed. Just that quickly I realized I barely knew the man.

My parents had kicked me out. Now Grant didn't want me either. Where was I supposed to go?

Three

The End of the Beginning

I couldn't get off the dining-room floor. The crushing weight of Christopher's declaration—and his emotionless departure—left me feeling cold and lifeless. No discussion. No compromise. Just the slamming of a door that seemed to say, "Good-bye…forever." Receiving news of his death would have been easier to accept than all of this.

I was overwhelmed by the reality that my son was gay and didn't want to change. Our family was broken, and my life was falling apart. Every dream I'd had for years—for my marriage, for my sons, for my future—was gone. I could see no more reason to live. I was certain that I'd have no satisfaction or happiness in this world. I saw only sadness, disappointment, and rejection. And I wanted no more of it.

I slowly pulled myself off the floor and went to the bedroom, where I sobbed until dawn. I was at the intersection of life and death. Death's road seemed less painful—so it was the one I chose.

I would end this misery that had started so long ago.

— — —

I was born in Shanghai and grew up in Taiwan. My mother worked outside the home as a politician and career woman, and she left my siblings and me to the care of nannies. My grandparents on both sides of my family had passed away. My father was a merchant marine, so we rarely saw him. Our home was nothing out of the ordinary, except for one thing—the absence of a mom and a dad. The more time my parents spent building their careers, the lonelier I became. I was envious of my friends whose mothers stayed at home, cooking, cleaning, and caring for their families.

Each day when the school bell rang, I'd walk home along the dusty streets with my next door neighbor, Mei-Lin. When we arrived at our homes, she'd open her gate and call out, "Mom, Mom! I'm home!"

I, on the other hand, opened the gate every day with no one to greet me. I'd go to my room and spend the afternoon alone, watching from my window as Mei-Lin's mother hung clothes to dry on the line behind their house. Mrs. Lin would bring out a homemade snack for Mei-Lin, and Mei-Lin would eat it while she sat on the step and watched her mother, arms full of clothes, shuffle around the yard. I couldn't help but scan our empty apartment, seeking the outline of my own mother. But she was never there.

At the age of nine, I vowed to be like Mei-Lin's mother—to be home when my husband and children were home. My life's work would be home, family, and my husband's career. I would build a different kind of life for my family and a home that was different from the one I grew up in.

When Leon and I first came to the United States in 1964, we were two young transplants on foreign soil, struggling to grow roots. We had no family here, no friends, and no money. Starting with nothing, we raised a family on meager financial resources. Leon got his PhD and his DDS, and I gave birth to two sons—Steven and Christopher. We lived on a very tight budget, but that didn't matter because we were building a future for our sons. Those days were full of hope and anticipation. I had a family—a place where I belonged—and I poured all of myself into it, expecting to find the joy and satisfaction I so longed for.

As school-age children, Steven and Christopher were both honor students and winners of piano and math contests. They were well behaved and obedient, but sadly, they often were ridiculed or bullied at school. They persevered, as we did, and friends and neighbors later praised us as model parents and frequently asked for parenting tips. We clipped enough newspaper articles about the boys' accomplishments to fill numerous scrapbooks. And on top of their honors and awards, Leon and I were succeeding in life. We had a thriving dental practice, and I took pride in our picture-perfect family. But I still felt empty. I was living a double life: successful on the outside, but empty on the inside. A hole gaped in my heart, and I ached to fill it. Family accomplishments, the things I worked so hard for, brought me no comfort.

As time passed, there was a crack in the pristine facade of my role as a mother. Our boys, now young men, changed dramatically. No longer were they my high achievers who earned honors and awards that I could take pride in. Instead, they lived carelessly and with no clear direction for their future. Our older son, Steven, left home after college and was living a hedonistic life. While his rebellion might be considered typical for an American fraternity boy, he certainly was not raised that way.

Christopher had been my last ray of hope; he was obedient, caring, thoughtful. But now this—his announcement a week after Mother's Day that he was gay. Christopher had rejected me, the family, and the life I had prepared for him. How could I not feel hopeless?

— — —

Throughout my sleepless night, Christopher's decision to walk away replayed over and over in my mind. *Every person I have ever loved has walked away from me. What else is there to live for?* I had contemplated ending it all before, but there was always something to hold on to: the boys, the dental office, our rental properties. But now none of that mattered. There was nothing holding me to this world any longer. So my resolve was firm: this would be the end.

With my mind made up, I felt the need to see a minister. I'd never been religious and actually had an aversion toward Christians, but I wanted someone to talk to before leaving this earth—someone who would listen. Maybe this was a good way to find closure. The problem was that I didn't know any ministers except for Father Foley, the chaplain at Loyola, where Leon taught once a week.

I walked into the kitchen, where Leon was eating breakfast. He acted as if nothing unusual had happened the day before. I stared at him for a second, amazed that he could be so calm when our family had fallen apart. I hesitated before speaking. "I want you to drive me to see Father Foley."

We rode in silence. Not a word was said about Christopher. Our years of noncommunication made silence the norm between us, and as always I was feeling completely alone. The meeting with Father Foley was short. He listened, I cried, and Leon did nothing. Father Foley was gracious and spoke comfortingly, but his words were not enough to resuscitate my deadened heart. As we were leaving, he put his hand on my shoulder and handed me a booklet. I thanked him for his time, all the while reconfirming the plan to end my life.

— ■ ■ ■ —

The next morning was cold and drizzly, but I left the house early and walked to the Metra train station. It would be a lot easier to take trains and buses to my final destination. I took only my purse and the booklet from Father Foley. I'd thought it through. Before I ended my life, I wanted to see Christopher one last time. His departure two days earlier had been too abrupt. I couldn't leave it that way. I would say a final good-bye in Louisville, then I would end it all.

I made it to Chicago's Union Station and asked the agent for a ticket on the next train. "Would you like a round-trip ticket?" the agent asked.

"No. Just one way," I said.

"But it's only three dollars extra," he pointed out.

"No thanks."

"You can use it anytime in the next twelve months."

"Really, I won't need it… I'm not coming back." Three dollars—not much—but at this moment my life wasn't worth even that much.

I stood in line, waiting to board the train, and looked around the terminal at the people coming and going. I saw a group of well-dressed, handsome young men in front of me. They talked and laughed, then one put his hand on his friend's shoulder. I took in a quick breath. Could they be gay?

I turned the other way. On the other side of the terminal, a train had just arrived, and passengers were streaming into the hall. A young man looked around and then started running—right into the arms of another man. I couldn't believe it. Had I been so oblivious before? And they all looked so normal—just like Christopher.

I boarded the train, and as we pulled out of Chicago, I actually felt some relief. I was on my way to the end of the road. Even though everything else in my life was out of control, at least I could control this one thing. I couldn't control what had happened to my life, but I could control the end of my life.

I was still holding on to the booklet I'd received the day before. Its cover was worn and the edges curled after being in my hands for so long. Finally, I looked at the title: *Homosexuality: An Open Door?*[1]

Interesting, I thought. I began to read.

It was a Christian booklet, but for the first time I didn't want to avoid it simply for that reason. I was captivated by every word. The booklet explained that God loves everyone—even homosexuals—because of who they are, not what they do. I had never heard this before. I had decided that I couldn't love my son anymore because of his decision. But this booklet said that God loves homosexuals—even Christopher—regardless of what they do. I thought that if God can love my son, then I could still love him as well.

As I continued reading, I realized that I wasn't reading it for Christopher. Even though it was written for people who had homosexual feelings, I felt like the booklet was written for me. It spoke about death, that death was the result of our brokenness, our failures, our imperfections. Instead of our dying, Christ died for us so that we wouldn't have to die. *I won't have to die?* But what was there to live for? Everything that I had ever loved had rejected me. If there was no love here for me, why remain?

Then I read a statement that seemed to pierce my deadened heart. Nothing can separate us from the love of God that is in Christ Jesus.[2] *Nothing? You mean God loves...even me?*

The train rumbled down the tracks on that May morning. I usually found traveling through Indiana's flatlands monotonous. But as I gazed out the window, it seemed like I could see for miles. The fields were bursting forth with new life as rows upon rows of crops seemed to extend to the horizon. All my life I had been an atheist and even despised Christians. But at that moment, as I was looking at the beauty of nature, I knew there must be a God.

A calmness came over me. The wonder and awe of the outdoors seemed to radiate through the glass and surround me. Then I heard a still, small voice that said, *You belong to me.*

I wasn't startled or scared. The voice was not loud, nor was it a whisper. But it seemed to be right next to me—gentle, sweet—as if it had been there all along. I felt the tension in my shoulders melt away, and my muscles began to relax.

All my life I wanted to belong. Belong to my parents. Belong to my husband. Belong to my children. But God was telling me that I didn't belong to anybody on earth. I belonged to him.

He knew my deepest need, and he spoke the words I longed to hear. Those four words were a healing balm to my shattered heart. I had not been seeking God, but I was found by him.

Suddenly it seemed possible that my visit with Christopher—the visit that I had envisioned as one last good-bye—might actually be the beginning of something new.

Four

Two Lives in Louisville

Christopher: May 18, 1993

The clinic was buzzing with noise as I entered a few minutes past one in the afternoon. I'd had a quick lunch, but somehow I still managed to be late. Most of my classmates were bringing patients back to examination cubicles, and some had already begun cleaning teeth and taking x-rays. The high-pitched whine of dental drills began to cut through the air, enough to make most patients cringe. But this was all part of a regular day for me. Not quite music to the ears…maybe more like *cha-ching*.

I cleaned my countertop, draped my chair with a disposable plastic cover, and donned my surgical gown. This ritual was part of a daily transformation from fun-loving bartender into serious, professional dental student. I laughed and thought, *If only my patients knew.*

Sure, most of my classmates knew I was gay. Several of them were too, not to mention one of my professors. But my patients didn't need to know. I wasn't "in your face" about my sexuality. I considered myself quite normal.

Normal was all I ever wanted to be, starting at a young age. To begin with, I'm Asian. All through grade school and into college, I was never fully accepted. I was sensitive, nerdy, and horrible at sports, and I loved music and the arts. So I was familiar with being different from others. In

I loved music and studied piano from the age of five until I was in college. This was taken in 1988, the year I graduated from high school.

dental school I was one of the gay students. But being different didn't mean I couldn't be normal. I wanted to be successful and respected. I wanted to settle down with someone and live happily ever after. My dreams were no different from the dreams of straight men and women who were in class with me.

I had hoped these things would happen with Grant. He was a lawyer and highly regarded in his profession. When he asked me to leave, he wasn't a jerk about it. He even helped me find a place to stay. One of his friends who traveled a lot needed someone to watch his house and feed the dog, so Grant suggested I move in. It was a newly renovated, three-bedroom ranch in an upscale, wooded neighborhood. For the time being, it was a nice setup—especially since it was free.

But it meant coming home to an empty house every day. I wanted company, somebody to talk to. I wanted companionship. Lying in bed alone at night had certainly not been part of my plan.

I walked to the counter in the middle of the clinic and gave the dental assistant my paperwork. In return she handed me the instruments I needed for this afternoon's appointment, wrapped neatly in blue autoclavable paper. I grabbed some latex gloves, stuffed a few extra pairs into my pocket, and headed back to my cubicle.

I set out the mirror and explorer on the plastic-covered metal tray by the patient chair and waited for my name to be called. Once patients arrived at the dental school, they would sign in and ask the receptionist to page their student dentist. My patients had been late before, so waiting was nothing new. Meanwhile, I had nothing to do but think. My mind drifted to the last few days: visiting my parents, telling them I was gay, their kicking me out…and then enduring Grant's rejection. The pain still pricked like a sharp needle from a shot of Novocain.

I had been so excited about moving in with him, and now I felt stupid and alone. There was nothing I hated more than being alone. I wanted to be like everybody else I knew—finding someone to love and building a life together. Now I was having to start over again.

— — —

I always dreaded a life of loneliness, but early on I knew that there was something very different about me. Several summers out of my childhood, my family would travel to visit friends in Iowa. The kids had been about my age, and their father had gone to college with my dad. We spent our days swimming in their pool and watching movies on cable television—something we didn't have at home. What my parents didn't know was that my father's friend kept *Playboy* and *Hustler* magazines under the sink in each bathroom. I was nine years old when I looked at those magazines for the first time.

My heart raced for fear of being caught, but also with excitement and curiosity. It was not the women who caught my eye—but the men. I was too ashamed and confused to tell anyone that I had these feelings. I feared my parents would punish me and the kids would ridicule me. So I hoped and hoped that these feelings would go away. But they never did.

Believe me, I tried everything I could to become "normal." I tried dating girls—only a handful—but they all dumped me. A girl in high school broke up with me because she was moving to Spain. A girl in college dumped me and went back to her old boyfriend. A girl in Chicago ended our relationship because her parents didn't approve of me. Each time the rejections hit harder and harder—especially since the relationships were my ticket to fitting in and being like other guys. But deep down I knew I wasn't drawn to women the way other men were.

Still, I wanted my sexual desires to change. I tried ignoring them; I tried suppressing them; I worked hard at focusing more attention on girls. None of it worked. So after years of secrecy and inner turmoil, I knew I couldn't deny my attraction to men. I just needed to accept this fact about myself.

After I moved to Louisville, I started going to gay clubs and began tending bar. Before I knew it, I was living a double life. By day I was a professional dental student. By night I was a popular bartender at a gay club. To me, it was a natural fit—at least for the time being.

— — —

"Chris Yuan. Chris Yuan, please come to the reception desk." The familiar voice crackled over the intercom system, snapping me back to the present. I headed to the reception area to greet my patient, but I didn't see him. So I walked over to the receptionist.

"Hey, Cathy. Who paged me?"

"I did." She shuffled some files as she looked up at me. "Some lady came to look for you and told me to tell you she'd be waiting outside. It was kind of strange."

"Hmm. Okay, thanks."

I walked out of the clinic area, down the stairs, and outside. Squinting into the sun, I could see a woman standing on the sidewalk, a petite lady with short brown hair. As I neared, she turned around.

Mom?

"What are you doing here?" I asked in bewilderment.

"Hi, Christopher." She took a step toward me and hugged me as she spoke. "I just came to tell you that I love you... I love you, no matter what."

I took a step back, escaping her embrace. This was the last thing I'd expected. Coming out to my parents was supposed to give me freedom. And freedom meant not having a mother calling or writing or coming to Louisville to look over my shoulder. It felt like my newfound freedom was already slipping away.

She was the one who had given me an ultimatum. She was the one who kicked me out of the family. Everything had been going as others told me it would...until now.

I looked at my mother and laughed. "You came all the way to Louisville just to tell me that?"

I expected her to respond in anger, but she didn't. She even looked different. I couldn't put my finger on it, but something had changed. She wasn't flying off the handle. She seemed peaceful.

"Christopher, I want you to know I love you, even though I don't agree with your choice. I am your mom and I will always be your mom—"

"Yeah, yeah, I know." I cut her off in midsentence and looked down at my watch. *My choice!* I thought. *She just doesn't get it.* "I really need to get back inside. My patient is probably waiting for me. Is that all you want?"

"I…I guess so," she said.

I turned to leave, then stopped. "When are you going back to Chicago?" I was hoping she would answer, "Soon, really soon."

"I don't know yet. I haven't made up my mind."

That was different. She always knew what was going on and what she was going to do next. She was always in control. And now she didn't have a plan? Something strange was going on, but I didn't have time for it.

"Whatever," I mumbled, then walked back up the stairs to attend to my patients. What could she be up to now?

Five

New Birth

Angela: May 18, 1993

I walked away from the dental clinic with a spring in my step. It felt good to see Christopher and tell him what I had come to say. After his coming-out ordeal, I was able to tell him in person that I loved him, no matter what. Finally, some light was peeking through the end of the tunnel I'd been living in. As I stood on a street corner waiting for the traffic signal to change, I abandoned the plan to end my life. But I wasn't yet ready to go back home to Leon. For the first time in a long time—possibly ever—I felt at peace. But I needed time alone, maybe an extended period of time, to decide what I would do next.

I checked into a nearby motel and started for my room, but remembered I had no toiletries—you don't pack when you're planning to end it all. So I walked to a drugstore and drifted through the aisles, putting a toothbrush, toothpaste, and soap in my basket. I kept replaying the conversation with Christopher in my head. "Whatever," was his parting statement. Just days ago, the flippancy of that remark would have set me off, and I would have spiraled into a pool of self-pity. But now I felt okay—maybe even good. I was starting to realize that I didn't have to let his bad attitude control me as it had before.

I reflected again on the message of the booklet Father Foley had given me. I longed to know more about this God who loved unconditionally. I had been so thirsty, so dry for such a long time. I wanted simply to belong to somebody…maybe to God. I wanted to learn more about him, but I wasn't sure where to start.

Back at the motel, I pulled out the booklet and flipped it over. There was a phone number on the back. I sat on the edge of the bed next to the phone, then picked up the receiver and punched in the number. I was unsure what to say if someone answered, but I put the receiver to my ear anyway and took a deep breath.

The man on the other end of the line was warm and friendly. I told him about the past two and a half days and began to cry as I relived the still-raw memories. As difficult as it was, I felt a little relief. Getting it out seemed to lessen the sting.

After listening to my story, the man said, "Ma'am, I know how difficult this must be for you, and I want you to know that you are not alone. But one thing that is really important for you to realize is that you can't change your son."

My spine went rigid as I wiped away my tears. I refused to accept what the man had just said. I would find a way to fix my son and make things right again.

"Sir, I—"

"This is the most difficult thing for parents to accept. But let me give you the phone number of a lady in Louisville who has experience with these issues and can help you through this." I grabbed a pen and paper and scribbled the number, then thanked the gentleman as I hung up the phone.

I took another deep breath and dialed again, hopeful that this woman might give me the answers I needed. A lady picked up the phone, and her soothing voice invited me to open up to her. Her name was Dee Binkley, and I briefly explained my situation to her. Without hesitation, she invited me to come to her house. I left the Travelodge and headed to the bus station. Two or three bus transfers and a long walk later, I stood at her front door. Fear gripped my heart. Was I ready to take the next step?

I paused before pushing the doorbell. A butterfly fluttered past, moving from the flowers on one side of the stoop to the flowers on the other. Finally, I pressed the doorbell and wondered what would happen.

Footsteps padded across the floor inside. The knob turned, the door swung open, and I was met by a pair of sparkling blue eyes. A tall, beautiful woman stretched her arms out to greet me. "Angela." Her voice was soft and warm. "Welcome. I'm so glad you called and delighted you made it."

I hadn't even crossed the threshold and already I was crying. It had been so long since anyone had been glad to see me. I didn't even know this woman, yet she met me with a hug and words of welcome.

"Come in," Dee said. Her voice was comforting and sweet—motherly. Her house was tidy and smelled of lilac. Gentle music played in the background. The living room was decorated with warm colors that made it feel like home—even to a stranger. Just walking into this house, I felt loved.

"Come and have a seat." Dee motioned to her sofa. "Tell me about yourself."

No words came. I just burst into tears again. The events of the last few days had come to a head, and I couldn't keep it in any longer. Her gentle and genuine concern had caught me off guard, and my emotions burst forth like water from a broken dam. Dee put her arm around me and patted my shoulder. "It's okay," she said. "It's okay to cry." She handed me a box of tissues as I tried to regain my composure.

Dee waited quietly, and finally I was able to speak, though my words were interrupted by choking sobs. I told her the whole story—how my marriage was falling apart and my sons were in rebellion. I told her how I had failed, how I feared losing all I had worked so hard to gain, how I had come to hate myself. I told her my son was gay and I had planned to commit suicide that day. Dee just listened.

Then I told her of the comfort I felt when I read the booklet Father Foley gave me—but I didn't really understand what it all meant. Dee's eyes glistened as she listened to me, never leaving my own. It seemed that my burdens had become her own. Even though I was a stranger, she treated me like a sister. She suggested that I start reading the Bible. When I told her I didn't own one, she took me to Wellspring, a nearby Christian bookstore, to buy one.

She offered to meet with me a couple of times a week—kind of like a mentor. She called it discipling. She promised to walk with me along this new path. I had no idea where this would lead, but at least I knew I wasn't alone.

— — —

A couple of days after I met Dee, I moved out of the Travelodge and into Kentucky Towers, a fully furnished, pay-by-the-week apartment. I knew I needed to be in Louisville for a little while longer. Something was happening inside me, and I didn't want to quench it by going back too soon to my old life in Chicago.

I hadn't called Leon to tell him where I was. He didn't try to track me down, so I knew he didn't care. I felt like Leon was vinegar on my heart. Even the thought of him was sharp and sour. It made my heart shrink.

At the apartment, I settled into a routine and began to read the books Dee gave me. I was able to sit and read for hours. Before, I had never been able to read for more than an hour or so without falling asleep. In fact, I got through college by making my boyfriends read my assignments and write my papers. But now I had such an interest to learn more about God. And as I read the Bible, I was beginning to learn more about myself.

Interestingly, as I focused on learning about God, my anxiety about trying to change Christopher started going away. I realized there was so much work left to be done in my life that I had little time to worry about changing my son. I was overwhelmed by the fact that I had been given a second chance. Everything I had thought and felt for fifty years was being overturned and replaced.

— — —

I contacted Christopher by phone that first week to let him know where I was and to keep in touch. I had been in Louisville only a few days when he told me he had received a letter from the dental school informing him that he was on academic probation. According to him, the school was being completely unfair; the associate dean didn't like him and, as a result, was out to get him.

So on the first Monday after I arrived, I went to the associate dean's office to try to get things straightened out. Surely the dean and I could have a talk and get Christopher's situation resolved. I was determined to see Christopher's reputation mended.

"I'm Angela Yuan, Christopher Yuan's mother," I said to his secretary. "Is Dr. Johnson in?"

"He's in a meeting now," the receptionist said. "Did you have an appointment?"

"No, but it shouldn't take long. Can I just wait for him?"

She told me I could sit in the reception area down the hall and she'd let me know when Dr. Johnson was available. Dee had assigned me two chapters from a book on spiritual growth, so I pulled my dog-eared copy out of my bag and flipped it open. I found a seat and started to read, determined to make the most of this time. That's when a strange word caught my eye: *shrikism*.[3]

The book explained that the shrike is a bird of prey that, after capturing its meal, impales it on a sharp object—a thorn or a twig—and tears it apart, piece by piece.

Kind of gory for a Christian book, I thought. The authors described a "human shrike" as a person who considers himself to be so righteous that he believes everyone else must be acting out of wickedness. In other words, "I'm always right and you're always wrong."

I shifted in my seat. *I'm almost always in the right. So isn't that a good thing? Doing right, being right?*

The book further explained that this type of personal righteousness attacks other people. It resembles the actions of the shrike—tearing something apart piece by piece.

That gave me pause. I thought back over my life, back to the times I'd insisted I was in the right and others were wrong. It had seemed so clear at the time, but now, with this new perspective, my actions didn't appear to be too far from those of a shrike.

In fact, that's what I'm doing here now—demanding fair treatment for my son.

The book explained that a person's attempt to prove his righteousness was the very thing that kept him from understanding God's love for him.

I began to see myself more clearly. I had come to the dean's office like a shrike—ready to show him that he was wrong and prove that I was right. I wanted to control the situation and not allow things to happen as they will. Suddenly, a realization formed deep within my soul, revealing something about myself that I had never understood before: I was a sinner. I was no better than Christopher or anybody else. I was horrified to recognize the darkness in my heart. And yet, as I understood my disease, I was able to understand the cure. Everything I had been reading for the last few days began to make sense to me. I was a sinner, just like a self-righteous shrike.

I stood up and closed the book. I didn't want to see the dean. I just wanted to get out of there. I shoved the book in my bag and discreetly walked to the door.

In order to get to the elevator, I would have to walk past the dean's office, and I was too ashamed to face him—or his secretary. So I snuck around to the stairwell and held my breath as I quickly but quietly tiptoed down the stairs. My heart raced at the thought that I might bump into someone on the way.

With each step I took, I was more convinced of my sin. But amazingly, it was freeing. I felt the acceptance of being loved by God despite my sin. It was actually invigorating!

When I pushed open the exit door, I was able to take in a deep breath. It was a beautiful, bright day, and I picked up my pace as I walked—almost skipped—down the sidewalk. I was rejoicing in the truth that I was far from perfect. I didn't have all the answers, and I never would. But it was okay, because I no longer had to be perfect. My Father in heaven loved me anyway. It was all I could do to keep from shouting, "I'm a sinner! I'm a sinner! I'm a sinner!"

Six

Don't Try to Change Me!

It was a warm May afternoon as I hurried down Fifth Avenue in downtown Louisville. My mother had just moved to Kentucky Towers, and I was meeting her for lunch. As I walked onto Muhammad Ali Boulevard, I could see the black awning extending from the dark brick building. I arrived at the front door slightly out of breath. A bead of sweat trickled down my face as I stepped into a small, musty-smelling lobby.

It took my eyes a moment to adjust to the dim interior. The building was old, with black floors and black walls. A tall doorman in a polyester suit stood behind a high counter.

"I'm here to see Angela Yuan."

He asked me to sign in, then pointed to the elevator lobby behind him. I felt like I was traveling back in time as I stepped into a small, old-fashioned elevator that crept up to my mother's floor.

"Hi, Christopher. I hope you're hungry," Mom said as she opened the door to her new place. It was nothing fancy, the carpet worn and the furniture old. I looked around the small apartment. She had brought very little with her from home. I saw a few groceries sitting on the counter, sandwiches and drinks set out on a small table, and some books scattered here and there. I noticed that my mother was wearing clothes I hadn't seen before.

"Mom, where did you get those clothes?"

"Oh…these are from the Salvation Army not too far from here. I didn't bring any clothes from home." She smiled as she walked to the dining table. "Let's eat. I know you don't have a lot of time. Besides, you must be hungry."

We sat at the small table, and I picked up my sandwich. I was about to take a bite when my mother asked, "Can we pray before we eat?"

Pray? My mother had never prayed before a meal. I wasn't sure how to respond, but in my hesitation my mother took my hand and began to ask God to bless our food.

"Amen," she said as she looked up and smiled. "I know that you like your bread toasted so it melts the cheese and butter. I hope you like your sandwich."

"Yeah…right," I said, taking a small bite. I looked at the stack of books sitting near the table. A spiral notebook and pen lay nearby, and the titles were some I'd never heard before. They seemed to be all spiritual or religious books, and at the very top was a thick book covered in black leather.

"Mom, is that a Bible?"

She looked at me. "Yes." She was the slightest bit hesitant.

I looked back at her, dumbfounded.

"I've been meeting with this lady who's Christian…" Her voice trailed off.

I was trying to figure out the angle. Was she trying to impress me or set a good example for me? I could have told her that "finding religion" wasn't an especially good way to do that.

I looked around the room and noticed other things that surprised me. Two twigs sitting on the windowsill were fashioned into the shape of a cross and held in place with a twist tie. Below the window on the floor was a small pillow with a box of tissues next to it. Alongside those was a notebook with *Prayers* written on it. There was a bookmark on top of the notebook that said, *For God so loved the world.* I looked back at my mom and realized she was wearing a cross.

What was going on? My mom had always hated Christians and religion. She could never stand religious hypocrites. The last thing my mom would become was a Christian. People in Chicago joked that if Jesus were to walk in front of my mom, she still wouldn't believe. This was getting way too bizarre. I scooted back from the table and stood up.

"What's wrong, Christopher?"

"Nothing, Mom. I just… I gotta go."

"Aren't you going to finish your sandwich? You haven't eaten anything."

"No…no, I need to run. I'm gonna be late getting back to school. I'll see you later, okay?"

"Christopher, wait, can I pray for you before you go?"

"Uh…you can pray for yourself, Mom. Bye."

I walked down the hallway to the elevator. As I punched the button for the first floor, I couldn't get the idea out of my head that something very strange was happening to my mom. I couldn't figure it out. But whatever it was, I didn't like it.

— — —

Several weeks later, I drove my mom to an area in Louisville that was unfamiliar to both of us. *I can't believe I agreed to do this,* I thought. I shifted my car into park, and my mom and I stepped out onto the sidewalk. We walked down a tree-lined street in a quiet, upscale neighborhood. It was dusk, and iron streetlamps lit our path. We were headed to meet Colonel John D. Jefferson, a retired marine who practiced law in Louisville. My mom had been told that Jefferson "knew a lot" about homosexuality. I told her I would see him, but I was dreading it.

We came to his building and opened the big oak front door. The colonel was waiting for us. He was a tall man—very fit—with perfect posture and a charming smile. He greeted us wearing a neatly pressed suit and a bright-red tie. One thing I must admit: I was impressed with his office. The styling was immaculate—dark mahogany wood, Civil War–era furniture, twenty-foot-high ceilings, and bookshelves from floor to ceiling. Photographs of his beautiful, blond-haired, blue-eyed family with their purebred golden retriever sat in expensive frames alongside legal volumes, the Bible, a bust of George Washington, and the American flag. *Who is his decorator?* I wondered.

He asked us to sit down, and as he leaned back in his chair, he smiled at my mom, then turned to me. "So, Christopher, your mother tells me about your most recent…decision."

I could feel my blood pressure starting to rise, but I held my tongue.

"I'm not sure you've fully thought this through, son. Your mother tells me you're a marine. So can I share something with you—from a marine to another marine?[4]

"Are you aware of the statistics about the gay…lifestyle?"

Deep breath. It took all that was in me not to roll my eyes. "What's that, sir?"

"Well, for one thing, gay men have a shorter life expectancy than straight men." He looked at my mom. "This has been proven by reputable scientists."

Reputable! You've got to be kidding. Was this what you'd call knowing a lot about homosexuality? Using skewed statistics to "prove" that gay men die sooner than other men? How could any researcher gather an unbiased, representative sample of gay men, when many don't want their sexuality to be known and others are still denying even to themselves that they are gay? Most of those studies only gathered data from gay men who died as a result of AIDS. What about all the other normal gay men?

He continued. "Did you know that a survey of gay men shows that most have had sex with someone under the age of eighteen?"

Seriously? Give me a break! None of my friends slept with teenagers. Did the survey clarify when it was that they slept with someone underage? Most likely they were teens themselves. And by way of comparison, what were the stats for straight men?

"Besides, God says that this is not normal. It is unnatural, and it says so right here in this book. It's called the Bible. All the answers of life can be found here."

He continued, saving the show-stopper for last: "Did you know that change is possible?"

Does he think I haven't tried? Does he honestly think I want to be this way? For years I had tried every way I could think of to be attracted to women. I had even prayed to God. But nothing I tried, not even pleading with God, worked to change me. *This is who I am. I'm as gay as I am Chinese. God created me this way.*

I couldn't change, and I knew that God didn't want me to change. I could never be straight. Why was it so hard for people like the colonel to realize that?

I tried to understand what was going on in this conversation, and I concluded that the colonel thought that by giving me messed-up statistics and repeating bad research, he would scare me straight. He expected me to say, "Wow, you're so right. I shouldn't be gay! It's so bad for me. I'll live such a sad and short life. I guess I'll just be straight now. Thanks so much, Mom, for bringing me here. Let's go home now so I can find a wife and start having babies!"

I wanted to speak, but the words seemed to be piling up in the back of my throat. There were so many things I could have said to refute his distorted reasoning, faulty logic, and inconsistent research. But to be honest, it wasn't even worth my breath.

So I turned him off. He babbled on about religion, the possibility of change, and something about a counselor who could help me. After a while, my mother thanked him for his time, and I left his office without shaking his hand. *What an idiot,* I thought.

As we walked back to my car, my mother asked if I was interested in seeing the counselor the colonel had suggested. I looked at her and said,

"No, but you might want to make an appointment. You're the one who needs a shrink, not me. Besides, if you've come to Louisville to try to change me, you're wasting your time." I got in the car and shut the door.

— — —

My mother remained in Louisville six weeks before my dad and older brother, Steven, came to pick her up. My mother wanted to go to a Christian conference near Lexington, only an hour and a half away, at a school called Asbury College. As it turned out, we all went. I still don't understand how she talked us into it. I guess it's a mother's power of persuasion.

As we approached the registration table, I noticed that the people standing around were quite strange—and yet a little too familiar. The guys were well dressed and overly friendly. The women had short hair and wore jeans and tennis shoes. It all made sense now. This was a conference for people like the colonel mentioned—gays turned straight. That's why my mother dragged me here. A few weeks earlier, I had suggested that she check out the local Parents, Families and Friends of Lesbians and Gays chapter, but she never went. And instead she dragged us to this? I looked at the sign behind the registration table: *Exodus.*

We were given name tags and invited into a large auditorium. We sat up in the balcony, away from the main crowd. The conference started with music, and the instant the guy at the front strummed the first guitar chord, Mom started crying. Not just a few tears, but gut-wrenching, body-shaking sobs. She was a complete mess, and it was so embarrassing. She kept it up even through the speaker's message. Fortunately we were in the balcony where nobody could see us. I couldn't wait to get out of there.

But after the main session, my mother wanted to attend a workshop for parents. So my brother and I went to another workshop on controlling your "homoerotic feelings." I looked around the room at men hugging one another and chatting. I felt like I was back in the Highlands, Louisville's gay section of town. As my brother and I sat at desks near the back, an especially flamboyant man pranced into the room and called out, "So is this the workshop where we learn how to be attracted to men?" The other men burst out laughing and motioned for him to sit with them. *Is this how it is when gay men are "cured"?* The guys in this room were gayer than a Broadway musical.

I knew plenty of men who were gay and not pretending they'd been transformed into heterosexuals. And my gay friends were nowhere near as effeminate as these men who were pretending to be straight.

"What a bunch of queens," I whispered to no one in particular. I could never do this—deny who I really was. *They're only fooling themselves.* My mom probably brought me here in the hopes that I might change. But it only reinforced the reality of what I was—a gay man. Only one thing got me through that day: the thought that my mom would soon go back to Chicago and get out of my life.

Seven

Baby Steps

The ride back to Chicago was so different from my journey to Louisville six weeks earlier. It seemed like I'd been gone for a lifetime. The woman who had boarded the train that headed out of Chicago was not the same woman who was returning. It's amazing how much can change in such a short time.

After leaving the Exodus conference, we dropped Christopher off in Louisville and jumped on the road heading back home. Few words were spoken during our seven-hour drive to Chicago. I wondered what Leon and Steven were thinking—especially since I'd been gone for six weeks. I had left home before, but not for this long, and never with such a drastic change taking place in my life.

I rested my head against the window as we headed up Interstate 65. Acres of farmland spread out in all directions. We drove for hours and saw nothing but open space, with an occasional farmhouse set back from the road. The farms seemed safe and strong, tucked away from the rest of the world.

For the past six weeks, I'd been like the farmhouses—simple and solitary. I'd been free of the stresses of running a dental office, maintaining a household, and managing our rental properties. Nothing demanded my attention, so I was free to focus on one thing—my new life in Christ. But as evening set in, I felt I was moving further from the new life I had come to love. I looked at Leon and realized I was scared to go home. I didn't want to return to the arguments, the rejection, the constant need to prove my value to others.

I was not sure I would be able to face life with Leon again. He grew up as an only son and was spoiled by his parents and sisters. His parents never corrected him and never disciplined him. So to him, confrontation was wrong and to be avoided at all costs. But I felt that confrontation was a normal and necessary part of life. Without healthy arguments, how could there be true intimacy? And as we pulled into our driveway, I knew a return to our familiar, hurtful ways was waiting. It would be the same pattern—the denial, the avoidance, and the uneasy silence.

Steven grabbed his bags and headed off to his apartment. I closed my eyes and clutched my seat belt with both hands. Leon got his bags and closed the trunk.

"Are you coming in?" he asked.

"No," I whispered. He went inside, and I stayed in my seat, not letting go of my seat belt. *If I just stay here,* I thought, *everything will be okay.*

Except for the rhythmic ticking of the cooling engine, the garage was as silent as a tomb. In the dim glow of the garage-door light, I saw the familiar sights of home—which would have been a comfort for most people returning from a trip. But they only reminded me of the life I had decided to end just a few weeks earlier.

No doubt Leon was headed to bed. He didn't seem to care that I was still sitting in the car. He'd be fast asleep before long.

To my left was the door leading into the house. Behind me, another door led outside—the door to freedom—which looked much more appealing.

Should I just leave this place? Does God really want me here, dealing with the stresses of this life, this marriage? I was at a crossroads. Should I stay...or should I leave? I knew which one would be easier, but I also knew which one I should choose. Did I have the strength to go through with it?

The ticking of the car's engine continued and was now accompanied by the chirping of a cricket, lost somewhere in the garage. I was still clutching my seat belt when the garage light clicked off, and I sat in darkness. The difficulty of my decision weighed on my heart as I fell asleep. My hands loosened their grasp from the seat belt and fell to my lap.

■ ■ ■

The morning light was shining through the edges of the garage door. I could hear cars driving down our street. Life outside had begun again. As warmth filled the garage, it called to mind a verse I'd learned in Louisville. "His compassions never fail. They are new every morning,"[5] even this morning. My life wasn't over; it was just beginning.

As I took a deep breath and reached for the door handle, I prayed, "Lord, give me strength to face this new day. Help me be the light of Christ in this family." I got out of the car and went into the house.

Once inside my familiar kitchen, I felt out of place. I felt like I'd been through surgery—my body bandaged from head to toe. My wounds needed time to heal. The pain was still too fresh, and I knew I wasn't in any shape to face the world. What I needed was a safe place, a sanctuary.

I walked into our master bathroom and noticed the four-by-six-foot shower stall. It was finished with large tiles, and it had a built-in bench seat in the back. Above the bench, a small nook had been built in as a shelf for shampoo and soap. The house was less than a year old, and we hadn't yet used this shower because we used another in the guest bathroom. As I looked at the shower stall, an idea came to me.

I grabbed my bag and hunted until I pulled out a cross I had made. I found the two sticks one evening when I was out walking in Louisville and bound them together. The cross fit perfectly in the little nook of the shower. I took out my Bible and set it on the bench. I found a small pillow and put it on the shower floor. The light above added a soft, warm glow to the stall as I got down on my knees in front of the bench—my new kneeling table. Looking up at the cross, I said a prayer of thanksgiving and began to feel a peace that things would actually be all right.

As I opened my Bible and began to read, I decided to make this my routine the first thing every morning. No matter what the day would bring, I would begin it in this prayer closet—just me and God. This would be my sanctuary. God knew exactly what I needed by providing this small haven in my own home. As I prayed I felt more than enough strength to get through this new day.

— — —

It was a warm July morning. I was kneeling in my prayer closet and reading my Bible when I received a phone call from Dee in Louisville. She and her husband were coming to Chicago to visit their son, who lived near us, and she wondered if they could stay with us. Without any hesitation I welcomed her and was more than excited to catch up with her in person.

When Dee and her husband arrived, I hugged her and introduced them to Leon. He was cordial—as he normally was—but also apprehensive. We showed them around our dental office on the first floor and our home upstairs. I showed them Christopher's room, where they'd be staying.

After they settled in, I brought Dee to my prayer closet. I had bought a few different Bible translations, including my main English and Chinese Bible, and they lay on the shower bench that was now my kneeling desk. I had multicolored pens and highlighters in a pen holder next to the Bibles. Sticky notes with different prayer requests covered the tiled walls. My first spiral notebook was full of notes, and on top of it I had a newer notebook, which was almost as full as the first.

I explained to Dee that since I had come back home, I'd begun meeting with a lady who had been mentoring me. This friend invited me to a

Bible study, but I wasn't ready to face people yet. I needed some time before I could take that step.

"Why don't you come to church with us on Sunday?" she said. "You know, baby steps." Even though I'd been a Christian for a couple of months, I hadn't yet set foot in a church.

"I don't think so," I said. "I still feel so weak. I'm not ready to go to church and socialize."

"That's not what church is about though, Angela. It's about worshiping God."

"But I'm so embarrassed. I don't know if I can meet people. And what if I see someone I know? I don't want to have to explain myself or have to explain about Christopher. I'm sure that people can see right through me and know what I'm going through."

"You're not going to see anyone you know," Dee said. "And no one's able to see what you're going through. Besides, I'll be there to make sure everything's all right. We're going to worship God and hear his Word preached. I think…no, I know that you will be blessed. Come on. Please, come with us."

I finally gave in and agreed to go. Now, they had to convince Leon.

Dee and her husband, Ben, had an idea. Knowing that Leon had been baptized Catholic in college, Ben volunteered to take Leon to an early Mass at a Catholic church. After Mass, Leon and Ben would join Dee and me for the morning service at the Oak Brook Christian Center.

As I took my seat in the church, I was surprised at how comfortable I felt. Musicians started to play while people continued to file in all around us—chatting and smiling and hugging one another. As I looked around, tears once again began to flow. I was happy and content. I finally felt at home. These were honest tears of healing and hope, and I was beginning to feel free from the shame and self-pity of the past.

Eight

A New Love

Christopher: August 20, 1993

It was like a fairy tale. I'd never had a more beautiful birthday party. Though it was late August, the night was surprisingly cool with a light breeze. Electric lanterns swayed from the rustling branches of big oaks, and the tinkling of wind chimes punctuated the friendly chatter of fifty or more guests. My friends were scattered across a beautifully manicured lawn on a small hill in Old Louisville.

These people had come to celebrate this special day with me. And at last, on my twenty-third birthday, I felt I had a place where I belonged. Three months had passed since my breakup with Grant, which now seemed like old news. I was living in the studio apartment of a big, beautiful old house in one of Louisville's historic neighborhoods—an artsy area where brick foursquare homes were surrounded by hundred-year-old trees. It was my landlord, in fact, who had thrown the party for me, and he had invited all my friends.

Looking across the lawn, I spotted Doug, a landscape architect who had a knack for finding guys who had recently come out of the closet. He was sipping a glass of Riesling and chatting with a guy I'd never seen before. The unfamiliar man was athletic and clean-cut, and he stood holding a beer in one hand. The muscles in his shoulders rippled under his T-shirt. It's an understatement to say he didn't fit in with the rest of the crowd. He was "All-American" while the rest of us were "Gay Pride." So when Doug stepped away to get more wine, I walked over to ask him about the new guy.

"Who's that?" I asked, feeling like a teenager at a school mixer.

"It's Kevin," Doug said. "He's something, isn't he? I met him through work—he's a landscape architect as well."

"Really," I said, glancing over at Kevin. "Is he family?"

"No," my friend answered, laughing. "He's not gay. Not yet, at least. His wife just left him for an old boyfriend, and we've been teasing him, saying that he's really gay and just doesn't know it yet. So who knows? He could be your next project."

Kevin looked our direction and smiled. Doug smiled back and waved. "Do you want me to introduce you to him?"

"Yeah, of course," I said. "No, wait a minute." I tucked in my shirt. I wanted to be sure all those hours in the gym wouldn't go unnoticed.

I followed my friend across the lawn. I had only a few moments to gather my thoughts so I would make my best first impression. The lights strung overhead added a warm glow, and I did my best to quiet the butterflies in my stomach.

"Kevin," Doug said, "meet the birthday boy."

"Hi, I'm Chris."

To my delight, Kevin seemed interested in me. I asked him about his work, and he told me about his specialty in designing landscapes. He asked about my school and the field of dentistry—and more important, he noticed that I worked out. We realized that we both went to the same gym. I explained that I was beginning to prepare for my first bodybuilding competition, and he offered to train with me. How could I pass this up?

A couple of hours later, Kevin and I were sitting in a partially hidden area in the garden. I had a pretty good buzz, but it wasn't from the wine and the beer. Kevin had been talking about one of his projects—for a rich client across town. I had just met him, but already I was in a trance.

Kevin looked around and said, "Looks like everybody's gone home."
The yard was empty except for a few stragglers saying their good-byes.
"Wow, yeah. I guess time flies, huh?"

He stood up to leave, and before I could get out what I wanted to say,
he said, "Let me give you my number." We laughed the awkward laugh
that comes with first attraction, and my hands shook a little as I reached
for his business card.

I woke up the next morning feeling a new enthusiasm for life, which
always seemed to arrive with new love. My evening with Kevin had gone
from innocent to flirtatious in just a few hours. Soon after that evening
we went to the clubs together, and he stayed the night. Even though I'd
only known him a short while, I knew he was the one I could settle down
with long-term. When I found out he had been staying with his sister
since separating from his wife, I invited him to move in with me.

Within a week we were unpacking his boxes in my apartment. As I
was making room for Kevin's things in my closets, I was also making
room for him in my heart.

— — —

Kevin was working for Doug at the time, building his clientele as a landscape architect. He worked long hours, especially during the busy summer and fall months. I was in school and usually got home around five
o'clock. I'd spend the late-afternoon hours looking through recipes, going
to the grocery store, and fixing dinner for Kevin so it would be ready
when he got home. After dinner, we'd go to the gym and work out, and
on weekends we served drinks together at the Annex.

Our relationship was going well, but my school life wasn't. As I
spent more time at clubs, my grades declined. I was already on academic
probation when I met Kevin, and then the associate dean decided to
dismiss me—which meant if I wanted to continue, I'd have to repeat my
junior and senior years. It was an emotional and drawn-out process, and
Kevin was there for me every step of the way. So despite my struggles

and frustrations academically, I was content—so happy to be in a steady relationship.

Kevin was generally a guy who didn't say much, and not knowing what was going on inside his head intrigued me. I was attracted to the mystery, and it was exciting to try to draw him out. He was easygoing and usually not very opinionated. But there was one issue he would not budge on: the Bible and homosexuality.

Kevin had grown up in a Christian family. When he was married, he and his wife went to church together, and he believed without a doubt that homosexuality was wrong. He insisted that according to the Bible, homosexuality was a sin—something I totally disagreed with.

"I was born this way!" I told him. "So were you. We didn't choose this. How can it be a sin?"

But Kevin was adamant. "No, Chris. You're wrong on this one. It's a sin, plain and simple. Besides, you know I don't like to talk about it."

"You've got to be kidding. God loves us and created us this way. He wouldn't create us and then say it's a sin! Why would God say it's a sin to be who we really are? And why would God deny our love?"

At that, Kevin would end the discussion. Even though I usually got my way in the relationship, on this one issue he refused to budge.

Other than that, however, we never really argued about things. That year—1994—was one of the happiest years of my life.

But in early December, almost sixteen months after Kevin and I met, my dream life took a devastating turn. He told me he was ready to "move on."

I stood in the kitchen, stunned. Had I heard him right? Where was this coming from?

"Chris, we've been together over a year. You're my first boyfriend, and I just think I need some space."

My heart dropped to my stomach, and I felt lightheaded. *This can't be happening.*

"I'm really sorry, Chris. If it makes you feel any better, this has nothing to do with you. Really."

I asked where he would go, and he said Doug would let him stay at his house. I had suspected there was something going on between them—more than just the landscape business.

Kevin picked up a few of his things, threw them into a gym bag, and left. I couldn't sleep that entire night, crying away all alone in bed.

In the morning I picked up the phone and dialed a number I hadn't called in a long time. My mother's. I bawled my eyes out as I told her the whole story—how happy Kevin and I had been, how unexpected the breakup had been, how much I hurt.

She mostly listened, then told me that she hurt for me. She babbled on about God, but it didn't really matter to me. I just needed someone who would listen. I had focused so much on Kevin that I didn't have many close friends left. But that all changed very soon.

— — —

It was mid-December, and strobe lights were flashing while people danced to the thumping club music. I could feel the beat in my sternum. I'd gotten together with some new friends, Phil and Eddie, who both had gone through recent breakups. We were the three musketeers, you might say, out on a quest of our own—"all for one and one for all" in the battle for our hearts.

"It's been ten days," I shouted over the music.

"Ten days since what?" Phil asked, as he straightened his Santa hat. "Remember, we promised not to talk about those losers."

"Yeah, that's right," I said, but my heart wasn't in it.

"Let's have fun tonight, okay? 'Tis the season to be jolly!" Phil took a sip from his cocktail.

"I can't believe Kevin didn't even give you an explanation," Eddie joined in.

"Yeah, and Doug is a total jerk. It's unbelievable that he asked Kevin to move in right away," I said.

"Seriously, this is killing my buzz," Phil interrupted. "I'm here to have fun, not talk about those idiots. Besides, how many times do I have to tell you? No talking about exes!"

Phil grabbed us and leaned in to talk. The *thump, thump, thump* of the dance music played overhead as he spoke just loud enough for the two of us to hear. "You want your buzz back? I know something that might help."

"What?" I asked.

"Ecstasy. Someone said there's a guy in back who's selling it. Want to try it?"

I wasn't sure if I had heard him right. Drugs had never been part of the club life for me. I loved to party, and many of my friends did Ecstasy. But I had never tried it. I'd smoked pot, but it wasn't my thing. I rarely even drank alcohol, though I had served up more than my fair share of cocktails as a bartender.

"Oh, I don't know," I said, trying to gauge Eddie's reaction. "I've never done it before."

"Me neither, but after all that we've been through, don't you think we deserve to escape and just feel good? It's a week before Christmas, so think of it as an early Christmas present to ourselves."

Eddie shrugged, and before I could object, Phil said, "Great. I'll be right back!"

I turned to Eddie and asked, "Are you sure about this?"

"If I just wanted to sit around and cry about Greg, or hear you cry about Kevin, we could've stayed home. But we're here, so let's make the most of it!"

Eddie and I joined Phil at the bar. Phil shouted over the noise: "Three bottled waters, please!" The bartender slid our plastic bottles toward us. Then Phil turned to face us. "Let's go to the bathroom," he said, pointing toward the far corner.

The three of us crowded into the same men's-room stall, and Phil opened his hand to reveal three small white pills. They looked so harmless…kind of like aspirin. No powder to snort up my nose. Nothing to light up and smoke. No needles.

We each took a pill from his hand and looked at one another. I lifted mine up first and said, "Cheers! To the three musketeers!"

"Cheers!"

"Cheers!"

We touched our pills together and put them in our mouths. As I opened the bottle of water, I winced at how bitter the pill was. Really, really bitter. Eddie made a horrible face as he swallowed his.

"How long does it take to kick in?" I asked Phil.

"They say it usually takes about half an hour."

"Perfect, because they're playing our song!"

We ran out of the bathroom stall as the chorus of "We Are Family" rang out over the loudspeakers. We hit the dance floor, put our arms around one another, and jumped to the music, laughing as we sang along.

A few more songs played as we danced our hearts out. Then before I knew it, I felt lightheaded and nauseous. I grabbed hold of the railing close to the dance floor and accidently knocked over somebody's drink. I closed my eyes as disco lights made the room spin. I began sweating profusely. I'd never felt that hot before. I stumbled over to the fan and nearly tripped over my own feet. Fortunately, a trash can was nearby, and a few times I felt like emptying the contents of my stomach into it.

Then for some reason the nauseous feeling left and a sensation like I had never felt before swept over me. My teeth began chattering, not because I was cold but because I was on sensory overload—the hyperstimulation of all five senses. I got a chill that went from the top of my head to the bottom of my feet and then back up. Words can hardly express what I felt.

The euphoric chills continued up and down my body, and I could barely keep my eyes open, yet I was fully awake. All my senses were heightened, and it seemed like every neuron in my body was on rapid fire. I rubbed my fingers across the skin of my arm, and my knees almost gave way, it felt so good. Goose bumps covered my body, and every hair seemed to stand on end.

I looked across the room at the lights moving across the floor and walls, and as they raced back and forth, they left trails of light like comet tails. The colors were so vibrant and lively I could almost taste them. I loved the lights. I loved the music. I loved my friends. I loved my life. I just loved...everything!

I had never felt anything like this before. It was phenomenal. It was like the puppy love I felt when I first met Kevin—but multiplied a thousand times. Who needed relationships? I had found something much, much better.

Nine

A Marriage Built on Sand

Angela: December 27, 1994

I stood up and stretched, then stepped out of my shower-stall prayer closet after my morning ritual of reading the Bible and praying. As I padded across the floor, I thought about the things I needed to get done on this Tuesday morning. Laundry was at the top of the list. I walked past the kitchen into Christopher's room and began to pull the sheets and pillowcases from his bed.

Christopher had driven home and stayed for two days over the weekend to celebrate Christmas with us. It was so nice to have the whole family together. But after just two days, it was obvious that he wanted to get back to Louisville. Still, I thought that he might have wanted to stay longer—especially after the phone call I received from him a few weeks ago.

It was unusual for him to call, and even more unusual that he was telling me about his former boyfriend, Kevin. My heart broke for Christopher. What mother wouldn't hurt when her child was hurting? I wanted to reach through the phone line and give him a big hug. I wanted to offer my shoulder for him to cry on. I wanted to be there for my son and let him know that things would be all right.

As he poured out his heart, I couldn't help but think—couldn't help but hope—that the pain of this breakup might be the thing that would bring Christopher to Christ. I wanted him to know that no person—man or woman—could ever fully meet all his needs. Only Christ could.

I threw his bed sheets into the washing machine, poured in detergent, and closed the door. The water began to spray into the machine as I walked to the living room, which was still decked out with Christmas decorations. I was troubled by Christopher's silence over the holidays. When he came home four nights earlier, the sensitivity and openness that he had expressed over the phone was gone. He didn't show any sadness. In fact, he acted as if nothing bad had happened in Louisville. I didn't ask him about Kevin, but I still sensed that something was going on under the surface.

— — —

When both of my sons rebelled against their upbringing and the things our family valued most, it was hard not to wonder whether Leon and I had failed them. We had never set a good example for Christopher and his brother. After thirty years of marriage, our unresolved issues seemed to define our life together. Leon and I had argued about anything and everything. As much as I tried to build a home, I failed to make it a safe home. I failed to make it a haven for our sons—a place where they could feel secure. It wasn't unusual for me to take the boys and leave Leon for a few days or a couple of weeks after a big blowup. A sense of irritation had underscored every moment of my life, and I felt Leon was responsible for my misery. If only he would change, I believed, I could have a happy life. Leon didn't have extramarital affairs; he didn't drink or gamble; he didn't have any expensive hobbies. He was just cold and disconnected.

As a parent, I never realized how much our arguments affected our children. When Christopher was five years old, I found a picture he had drawn. He drew a boxing ring with Leon and me in the middle. On one side of the ring were Leon's parents and on the other side were my parents—and both sides were cheering on the fight. In the stands were two little boys with tears streaming down their cheeks. It was almost too much for me to bear.

My parents did not approve of Leon because his father was in the military and not very wealthy. They didn't think he was a good match for me, since they wanted me to marry someone with a higher social standing. However, I insisted on marrying Leon. When I went against my parents' wishes, my father slapped my face—the first and only time he ever did that. This was the ultimate form of humiliation in Chinese culture. But I believed that what I had with Leon was real; love could conquer all.

I was buoyed by Leon's parents' emotional support—at first. They loved the idea of Leon marrying me. While we were dating at Tunghai University in Taiwan, his parents praised me, saying how wonderful it would be if I married Leon. They believed I was the result of all the good fortune passed on from the Yuan family's ancestors. A fortune-teller even told them that I would be an excellent helping hand for a husband. But all that changed when we came to America and were married.

Leon was the first of his family to move to America and the only one to go to graduate school. He rode fifty-three days on a cargo ship from Taiwan, through the Panama Canal and up the East Coast to Ellis Island in October 1964. I followed a few months later, arriving first in Los Angeles. Eventually we were married in New York on September 11, 1965. It was a simple ceremony in a Catholic cathedral near Central Park. We chose that day because my father's merchant ship was docked in New York Harbor that weekend—and it just so happened to be my birthday. However, I didn't have the courage to tell my father beforehand that we were getting married. When he arrived in New York, he had no choice but to give me away on my wedding day.

Chinese tradition held the groom's family responsible to pay for the wedding celebration. So, later that same month, Leon's family arranged for a banquet in Taiwan, where the rest of our families were living. Leon and I couldn't travel back to attend the affair, but later we heard all about it. Toward the end of the evening and after many bottles of wine, Leon's mother stood up to speak. "My son," she began as she looked in the direction of my mother. "My son was once a pious son. After he married Angela, he is now a traitorous son." The people in the room stared at my mother with scorn. She wanted to dig a hole and crawl into it. When I heard about this, I couldn't believe it.

I can only assume the change in Leon's parents was due to the fact that he wasn't able to send money home the first year after he left Taiwan. He worked as a busboy most of that year before starting his PhD program at Stevens Institute of Technology in Hoboken, New Jersey. He began his studies the same month we got married. We were barely able to pay the rent, but we still sent money home. My in-laws thought that America's streets were paved with gold and that money grew on trees. So they expected Leon to send them a lot of money. When he didn't, they concluded that I must have spent all the money or prevented Leon from sending it.

I tried my hardest to please them. I passed up a full-ride scholarship to the University of Kansas in order to support Leon through school. I worked as a bank teller, making only about $250 per month before tax, and each month I would send $50 to my parents and the same amount to Leon's parents. But the money was never enough. Leon's parents continued to scold him for being a disobedient son. They even said that paying rent and paying tuition were not important. According to them, sending money home to Taiwan was the most important thing, because how else could we show our love for them? I tried to make things better by writing to them, but they wrote back and said they wanted letters only from their son.

There was tremendous pressure on Leon, and he caved in to his parents' unrealistic expectations. He wanted to be an obedient son above all else, because according to his mother and father, people who were disobedient to their parents deserved the deepest part of hell. So even though his parents didn't need it, Leon would want to send more money overseas, which meant less money for our food and necessities from our already-limited student budget. This led to arguments between us, but Leon would just grab the checkbook and send another check to his parents. Every letter that Leon wrote started with these words: *I know that I am a guilty and betraying son...* This broke my heart.

What made matters worse were the words that came out of Leon's mouth when we argued. He once said, "No matter what you do—no matter how hard you try—as long as my mother is alive, you will never be a good wife." He also told me how his mother would always remind him, "In life, you only have one mother. But wives are like paint on a wall." I could never understand the reason behind his cruel and cutting words.

Before our wedding I was sure we would have a picture-perfect marriage. But after the first month, all we did was argue. And when we didn't argue, Leon chose silence over relating to me. You might think silence was preferable to arguing, but I was starving for the love, attention, and support of a husband. On the day Christopher told us he was gay and walked out of our house, I was hoping Leon would finally step up and do something. This was his own son who was walking away.

But he remained silent. At the time of my deepest hurt, Leon turned away from me. It wasn't until I came back to Chicago after spending six weeks in Louisville that we began to talk about our hurts and struggles. Finally, we were beginning to look at the core issues in our marriage, the issues we had ignored for decades.

After Dee and her husband took us to church, I continued to go. Leon accompanied me and, to my surprise, began to open up to the gospel. In addition, he agreed to meet with a pastor, where we began to talk about our marriage. It was during one of those sessions that the pastor sensed the pressure Leon was under to be loyal to his mother. He asked

Leon point-blank, "Imagine that your mother is sitting in this room right now. Could you tell her that you love your wife? Could you tell her that Angela has been a good wife to you?"

My heart caught in my throat. I didn't know how Leon would answer, and I was surprised that the pastor was so blunt. Leon looked at the pastor and then dropped his head. "No," he said, voice wavering. "No, I couldn't."

Although it hurt me to hear him say this, I actually felt a little sense of relief. For so many years, I had felt like I was less important to Leon than his mother. We never openly talked about it, and when I tried to bring it up, Leon would erupt in anger. But now, in a pastor's office, we were able to get things out in the open—without arguing, without rage. Leon was beginning to change, and I was changing as well.

In the fall of 1993, Leon began attending a Bible study called Bible Study Fellowship, and it was there that he surrendered his life to Christ. He no longer looked at the Bible as simply a book written by men; he saw it as the Word of God. God softened his heart, and slowly he saw the need to be the spiritual leader of our home. He also realized that he was responsible to be not just a provider, but also my protector.

I began attending Bible Study Fellowship as well, and the teaching leader became my mentor. She taught me grace and patience through her own walk with God, and she pointed me to Scripture and prayer. Muriel was a prayer warrior who committed to pray for me, Leon, and Christopher. Her husband became close with Leon, and they helped us work through our many issues and walked with us along our journey of healing.

Leon and I had come a long way in our relationship. Now, communication was something we no longer avoided or feared. Sure, we still had our disagreements, but we were learning to pursue compromise and seek out good resolutions to our differences. By God's grace, divorce was no longer an option, when before it had seemed like the only way out. No matter how much we disagreed, we knew that God had brought us together in marriage and had made us "one flesh." Even though this was far from my childish, fairy-tale dream, I would still have had it no other way.

— — —

Dinggg. The bell on the washing machine signaled that the load was finished. I got up from the sofa and breathed a sigh of relief. Having hope really made life much more bearable—and sometimes actually enjoyable. I passed by our family picture, taken several years earlier, that hung on the wall. Things were so different then between Leon and me. We had looked good on the surface, but I had been so miserable. *Now,* I thought, *now, there's hope between us. We have a future that actually looks good.*

I peered at Christopher in the picture. I only wished I knew what the future would hold for my son.

Ten

Open for Business

Christopher: December 30, 1994

I felt my front pocket to make sure the cash was there. Six fifties. I stuffed the bills down and pulled my hand out to knock on the apartment door. It swung open, and a voice said, "Yo, Chris! Come on in, bro!"

"Hey, Brad. Thanks for letting me come by."

"Yeah. No sweat, man."

The apartment didn't look like a drug dealer's place. It looked like a regular bachelor pad with a sofa, a couple of chairs, and an open bag of chips and a can of soda on the coffee table. Some dirty laundry was scattered around the floor. I knew Brad from the Powerhouse Gym, the place I went to work out. But this was the first time I'd seen him outside that setting. He was wearing cutoff jeans, a T-shirt, and flip-flops. *This is what a drug dealer looks like?*

"In the market for some superman, are you?" he asked, showing me the Ecstasy on his counter.

I nodded, looking over the drugs.

"It's thirty a hit."

"Thirty dollars," I repeated. "And is this the good stuff?"

Brad nodded. "It's the good stuff."

"How pure is it? How long will the high last? I wanna make sure I bring in the New Year right."

Brad looked at me sideways. "Man, are you doubting me? You know me better than that. I'd never sell bogus stuff. Trust me, dude. This is the good stuff."

"Tomorrow's a big night, and I just wanna make sure I get good value for my money."

"Well," Brad chuckled, "I guess your mama raised you right."

"She did," I said, "or at least she tried."

"I know you'll like it," Brad said. "You won't do much better in Louisville. My Ecstasy is from the West Coast—where all the good stuff comes from. You'll roll all night, and it has some great trailer visuals when you're on the dance floor. And the comedown is nice and easy. You'll have an incredible New Year's celebration."

I pulled out the fifties. "Would you sell me ten hits for $250?"

Brad whistled. "You goin' into business for yourself?"

"Don't worry—I won't step on your toes. I'm just trying to cover my own expenses. Besides, I think you've got the straight scene covered at the gym. And you never go where I usually go…unless you wanna start." I smiled at him, then added, "But I think the guys at the Connection will be too intimidated by a big, straight musclehead like you."

"That makes sense. And you know, I'm not into that kinda stuff." He meant being gay. "But I see that you're a fast starter. From first-time user to buying in quantity, what, within a couple of weeks?" He laughed. "Sure, I'll sell you ten for $250. I'm always glad to get inventory out the door. Consider it my late Christmas gift to you."

Brad counted out ten white tablets and put them in an envelope. He handed it to me and pocketed the money. As I was opening the door to leave, he called behind me, "You know, if you can pay cash for a hundred hits, I can give you an even better deal."

So began my career as a drug dealer. At first my goal was just to get a slight discount and make enough to pay for my own habit. If I paid $250 for ten hits, I could sell nine of them for $270. That meant the tenth one was free, with a $20 profit.

The Ecstasy sold like hot cakes. I'd been working in the clubs for so long I pretty much knew everybody. I had an outgoing personality and had always been a natural marketer and businessperson. Before the weekend partying even started, I'd sold all nine tablets. So a few days later I was knocking on Brad's door to buy twenty more hits. When those were gone, I bought more.

When my student loan check arrived in January 1995, I was ready to make my first big purchase. I cashed the check and took a couple thousand dollars to Brad. He gave me a hundred hits of Ecstasy. My drug-selling enterprise was starting to gain momentum.

Before I started using Ecstasy, I'd get tired by four o'clock in the morning, when the clubs closed. But on Ecstasy, I had the drive to go to after-hours parties until daylight. At first I had said I would only take drugs on Saturday. But within a few months, the partying started to spill over to Friday night. Then Sunday. I spent little time studying and going to class. Getting to class on time was no longer a priority. The dental school administration contacted me and said I had to start signing in at the dean's office every morning when I arrived and every afternoon when I got back from lunch. They wanted to know I was there. But I wouldn't even do that when I did show up for class or for my patients. It was too much of a hassle.

While my academic life became less important, my drug-dealing career grew exponentially. Weekend road trips to party in Nashville and Atlanta introduced me to more drugs—cocaine, ketamine, acid, mushrooms, and crystal methamphetamine. It wasn't just Ecstasy anymore. Drugs—both taking them and selling them—became my life.

— — —

It was Memorial Day weekend in 1995. I was caravaning to Pensacola, Florida, with friends from Nashville. Thousands of gay men were flying in from all over the country to turn the Pensacola beach and Pensacola Civic Center into a gay mecca. By the time we arrived on Thursday afternoon, the beach was packed for miles with men—shirtless, tanned, and buff.

Lining the beautiful, white-sand beach were hundreds of huge tents elaborately furnished with sofas, chandeliers, wet bars, fountains, hot tubs, and even mini dance floors outfitted with their own disco balls. From huge speakers blared the familiar strains of the Weather Girls:

It's raining men! Hallelujah!
It's raining men! Amen![6]

I had never seen anything like it before. Thousands and thousands of gay men, all in one place, all having the time of their lives. And we hadn't even gotten to the main event yet. The big party was Saturday night at the civic center. The streets of Pensacola, normally a pretty sleepy place, thronged with young, gay men.

Outside the civic center, a group of Christian protesters had gathered, shouting at people as they filed in, shaking their Bibles and holding up signs that read,

Turn or Burn!
You're an Abomination!
Leviticus 18:22

I couldn't believe the audacity of these Christians. They had the nerve to come here and condemn me! I wanted no part of their stupid religion or their God who condemned me simply for being who I was. The hate I saw in their faces actually made me feel sorry for them, living in such ignorance. As we walked to the arena, we were laughing, making fun of the holier-than-thou protesters. But Sheena, one of the straight girls who partied with us, approached the protesters with a warm smile.

"Thank you so much for being out here and for caring about our well-being," she said.

The sign wavers were a little taken aback by her approach. Sheena took the hand of one of the protesters, a woman standing at the edge of the sidewalk. "Would you pray for us?" she asked the woman.

At first the protester didn't know what to say. But she soon recovered. "Yes...yes. Of course I'll pray for you."

"Thank you so much," Sheena said. As she started to bow her head, she asked, "Would you pray that the DJ will be twirling? Would you pray that there are lots of cute guys on the dance floor? Would you pray that my drugs really kick in and I have a perfect party buzz?"

The protester dropped Sheena's hand and recoiled. We laughed hysterically and continued into the building.

The name of the Pensacola party that year was Big Top, and it had a circus theme. The main entrances to the dance floor were supersize clown heads. Entering the mouth of the clown, I could feel the music. I didn't just hear it. I felt it. The sound system was perfect; the music was loud without being earsplitting. Nothing like Louisville or Nashville.

The dance floor was simply overwhelming. Huge, muscular dancers stood on pedestals, high above the crowd, and thousands of bodies, most with shirts off, gyrated to the music. Bars lined the outer edges of the bright and colorful dance floor, and bartenders sold mostly water to dehydrated partiers—high on Ecstasy—who danced and laughed with acquaintances and strangers alike. All around me people were hugging and having happy reunions with friends they hadn't seen since the last circuit party they'd attended.

As I snaked my way across the dance floor, over and over again unfamiliar but friendly faces said, "Wanna bump?"

"Sure." I'd lean down to snort a dab of white powder from the tip of a guy's thumb or a bumper on top of a small glass vial. It was either cocaine or ketamine; I never really knew what I was getting, but it rounded out my Ecstasy high. Everything here was so much bigger and better than what I saw in Louisville. Standing in the middle of the convention center floor, I spread my arms wide and said, to nobody in particular, "This is heaven!"

— — —

Back in Louisville, I ramped up the scale of my drug business so I could afford to travel to more circuit parties. On the weekends I was jetting off to Los Angeles, Montreal, Miami, New Orleans, or San Francisco. My classmates—the ones who were actually doing their course work and trying to live on their student loans—marveled at my lifestyle.

I met gay porn stars and male models. It seemed that every time I passed a magazine rack, I'd recognize the man on the cover of *Men's Health* or *Men's Fitness.* In only a few months, I came to think of Louisville as the place where I bided my time and made a little money selling drugs until it was time to fly off to the next circuit party. I had moved to the level of nouveau riche. The friends I made were hotter and richer and—in my mind—more interesting than those from the small-town scene in Louisville.

I started spending even less time in Kentucky and more time out of town. In August 1995, I was at the Saturday-night main event party during the weekend of the Hotlanta River Expo—Atlanta's annual circuit party. While dancing on one of the podiums on the dance floor, I met Ed Dollwet—or Mr. Ed, as everybody called him. Ed was from Los Angeles, and he had some great Ecstasy. He was known at the circuit parties for good, quality Ecstasy, and he made it a business, complete with business cards and a nationwide toll-free pager.

Ed and I hit it off immediately as friends—and business partners. The next day, I went to his hotel room at the Sheraton Colony Square on Fourteenth Street and bought a couple hundred hits of Ecstasy from him. After I returned to Louisville, he would mail Ecstasy and ketamine to me through FedEx, and I'd send him a money order. I also began to accompany him at several other circuit parties, where he would supply the drugs and I'd sell them. It was a great setup.

Since Ed's Ecstasy looked like mints, I kept them in Altoids boxes— just in case the wrong eyes were watching. There's nothing too unusual about a man giving a friend a mint on the dance floor. Then when Ed's Ecstasy became small white capsules, I changed to Tic Tac boxes, and "Can I have a Tic Tac" became our club code for Ecstasy.

Using all I'd learned about business from my father's dental practice, I began to run my operation like a business. I kept thinking, *How can I be more successful at this?* Following Ed's standard practice, with every drug transaction I made on the dance floor, I'd hand out a business card with my nationwide toll-free pager number. "If you get back home and need something—anything," I said, "just give me a ring." Suddenly, thanks to Ed and FedEx, I was nationwide. My beeper went off at all hours, day and night.

My apartment—the one where I used to study for dental school—became a mail-order fulfillment center. I could fill any size order. Two hits of Ecstasy to North Carolina? No problem. When I get your cashier's check, you get your drugs. Eight vials of ketamine to Ohio? It's in the mail. An ounce of coke to Colorado? No sweat! You'll get it in time for the weekend. I was selling to friends and new acquaintances from around the country, some dental school students in Louisville, and even one of my professors!

I was leading a double life—or at least trying to. By day I was supposedly a dental student. But by night, I was an interstate drug dealer. But what I loved the most was my night gig. Fame, fortune, drugs, and sex. What else could a person want?

— — —

In the late fall of 1995, the phone rang in my apartment. I picked up the receiver.

"Hello?"

"I can't talk now. But you need to know you're being watched."

I thought I recognized the voice of one of my Nashville friends, but the person was so panic-stricken it was hard to tell.

"Gotta go."

Click.

My heart began to race. I looked around my apartment. Anybody who raided my place would have caught me red-handed. Baggies, scales, spatulas, cutting dishes, shipping supplies—and, of course, illegal drugs. I had a bunch of Ecstasy and half a case of ketamine, along with a little cocaine and crystal meth.

I imagined a pair of DEA agents, wearing sunglasses and earpieces, in an unmarked car parked across the street, watching my every move through binoculars. I quickly turned off the lights and looked out the window. A few cars lined the street. Any one of those cars could be them. I closed all the blinds, then found a big duffel bag and stuffed all the drugs and paraphernalia into it.

I carried the bag to my car, terrified that I was being watched. *Be cool,* I told myself. *Just be cool. You're putting a duffel bag in a car. People put duffel bags in cars all the time.*

I drove a mile to the dental school on Preston Street. Nobody seemed to be following me. I circled the block. No, I was pretty sure there was nobody following me. I parked in back, pulled the bag out of the back- seat, and lugged it up the steps and into the building. It had been a while since I had opened my locker, but fortunately I still remembered the combination. I opened it, stashed the evidence, and walked, trembling, back to my car.

Then nothing happened. Every night I expected a knock on the door, but there was nothing. Every time I drove my car, I watched the rearview mirror for flashing lights, but I didn't see any. Whenever I saw a stranger around my place, I wondered if he was a drug agent.

After the mysterious phone call, I was on my best behavior. I quit selling drugs in clubs. I quit answering my pager. I started going back to class and studying. What else was I going to do with my time? Partying was out of the question until this thing blew over. When nothing hap- pened, I began to wonder if it had been a prank call. But the caller seemed genuinely freaked out.

One morning about two weeks after the phone call, I was late for school, perhaps driving a little too fast through a twenty-five-mile-per-hour zone on Louisville's medical campus. Just as I got to a stop sign, a car swooped around me from behind and turned in front of me to block my path. Two other cars screeched to a stop on my left and behind me.

Blue lights started flashing, and two men jumped out of their cars. I got out of the car, and they began yelling, "Don't move. Put your hands up!"

"What's the matter, officer?" I asked, knowing I might have been driving a little too fast. But thinking, *Isn't this a little over the top for a traffic stop?* As innocently as I could, I asked, "Was I speeding, sir?"

"Are you Chris Yuan?"

How on earth do they know my name?

"Yes," I said.

"We'd like to talk to you. You have the right to remain silent. Anything you say can and will be used against you in a court of law. You have the right to speak to an attorney…"

I tried my best to stay calm. *Are they reading me my rights? What's going on here?*

"Sure, why not? What would you like to talk about?"

"We have reason to believe that you are distributing amphetamines," one of the officers said as he turned me around and placed my hands on top of my car.

"Oh really? Wow, me?" I shook my head in dismay and gave my best look of innocent confusion.

One officer began patting me down while the other searched the car. They shook their heads as if to say, "Nothing," and they went on with the questioning.

"Do you know Ed Dollwet?"

"Of course. We've been dating since August." I'd never been a good liar, but I was getting better at it. They must have known I knew Ed. Better for them to think he was my boyfriend than my drug supplier.

"Do you know he's a drug dealer?"

I looked at them and gasped. "Ed? Are you sure?"

"We don't have a warrant to search your apartment. Would you be willing to voluntarily let us search it?"

"Of course," I said, laughing to myself, since I knew it was clean. "Do whatever you need to do. Are you sure we're talking about the same Ed Dollwet?"

I signed the release, and the police followed me home. They brought in drug-sniffing dogs, which worried me. I was afraid they would smell some drug residue and go crazy. But they came up empty. All they found were sex toys and piles of pornography. I was silently cracking up at the shocked looks on the officers' faces.

The police thought they had me dead to rights, but the apartment was drug free. They apologized as they left, and I was gracious about everything. But I could afford to be gracious. I had them beat. Not only that, but things would be easier now. What judge would give those guys a search warrant anytime soon, after I had submitted to a voluntary search and they found nothing?

I was untouchable.

Later that day I went to fetch the duffel bag from my locker at the dental school. I was back in business, with plans to expand.

Eleven

Let Go, Let God

Angela: March 19, 1996

The phone rang as I finished the paperwork for one of Leon's patients. I picked up the receiver, and my heart skipped a beat as I recognized a familiar voice that I hadn't heard in a while.

"Mom, I'm in trouble with school again." Christopher's troubled tone came through the phone line.

"What happened now?"

"They want to expel me. I'm meeting with Dr. Johnson next week. He said I'm out of second chances."

I could hardly breathe. "You said 'expelled.' Do you mean dismissed? Like before?"

"No, Mom. Expelled."

"But we just got a letter about your graduation," I said. Just last week, Leon had received an invitation to be part of the graduation ceremony and place the doctoral hood on Christopher. We were making travel arrangements, planning to attend the commencement ceremony in a couple of months.

"I know. Can you believe that I just ordered my cap, gown, and hood?" Christopher asked. "But it doesn't matter anymore. The associate dean has had it in for me since I got here. I'm gone."

"But you've already passed all your national board exams."

"Except the regional licensing boards," said Christopher. "And you can't take those until you graduate. So if I can't graduate, I won't get my doctorate. If I don't have my doctorate, I can't get my license. If I don't have a license, I can't practice!" His tone wavered between self-pity, self-righteousness, and anger.

"Can you believe they're doing this to me? And I'm so close! I guess when you're the associate dean, you can do whatever you want. They could have done all this sooner, but then they wouldn't have gotten four years of tuition out of me. Now there's eighty thousand dollars in student loans down the drain! How am I supposed to pay those back if I can't practice dentistry?"[7]

I sat in silence as I realized my dreams for Christopher were drifting away. I'd wanted to be a grandmother to his children; that would never happen. I had hoped he would work in our new office as a dentist; now that possibility was gone too.

So many times I had prayed, *Lord, do whatever it takes to bring this prodigal son out of that far country to you.* Maybe this was the answer to my prayers—the rock bottom I was waiting for. Could this be the one thing that would cause Christopher to surrender to Jesus? Still, my heart broke to see him going through this. And to think of him without any career, degree, or future—my soul ached just thinking about it.

"There are so many students in school who are worse than me," Christopher started up again. "This is a personal vendetta... Dr. Johnson hates me... It's so unfair!" Christopher's voice took on a different tone—not of remorse or repentance, but one that was shrewd, even deceptive. "You know, Mom, a few years back there was another student who was also going to be expelled. His dad is a dentist. Pretty well connected in the dentistry world."

I had an idea where this was going.

Christopher continued. "The guy's dad came down here and demanded to speak with Dean Robinson, Dr. Johnson's boss—and he threatened to sue the school."

I was uncomfortable with the tone of Christopher's comments, and yet this was his future. Leon and I sacrificed so much to come to America so our children would have a better life. "You know, Christopher, a lot is at stake here. I need to talk with Dad about this. Can I call you back later? Will you answer the phone this time?"

"Sure, Mom. Of course I will."

As I hung up the phone, I didn't know what to do. Any good Chinese parent would do everything in her power to ensure an excellent education, a noble career, and a solid future for her child. But I wanted to do what was right. I wanted to do what was God's will. But what was God's will?

I started fasting and praying, asking God for wisdom and discernment. I had no idea what it would look like, but I had a clear sense that Leon and I needed to step aside and get out of the way so that God could work in Christopher's life.

— — —

A week later, Leon and I flew to Louisville to meet with Dean Robinson. It was the same waiting room I had been in almost three years earlier, but this time my interior landscape was dramatically different. The last time I sat there, I wanted to fight for Christopher and prove the associate dean wrong. Self-righteousness consumed me. But on this day, I felt a calmness that I didn't have before. God was going to work this out as he had always promised.

God really had brought me a long way in just a few years. In the past, I would have been full of shame that my son was in such trouble with the school. But since coming to Christ and realizing my own brokenness and need for forgiveness, I knew that Christopher's rebellion was really no different than my own sins. It was just that Christopher's were more obvious. We're all sinners, and knowing that helped me stop worrying about what other people thought.

In the waiting room, Leon and I sat next to each other and across from Christopher. Wearing a suit and tie, he was looking his best, hoping to make a good impression on the man who had the authority to end his dental career before it even got started. Christopher was tense—I could see it in his face as beads of sweat gathered on his forehead. But he acted as if he would win this battle with the school, especially now that his parents were at his side.

Leon, after all, had taught at Loyola's dental school before it closed in 1993—and was now considered an adjunct clinical instructor at Louisville's dental school. He knew one of the associate deans here, a man who had moved down from Loyola. It wouldn't be hard for Leon to put pressure on the administration—enough pressure to let Christopher graduate with a DMD in May.

The room was silent, except for the ticking of a clock on the wall. More waiting. It seemed that I was always waiting. Before, waiting would drive me crazy, and I would strive to do whatever it took to make things happen. But now I began to appreciate the discipline of waiting. A few days ago during my morning quiet time, I read in Psalm 46: "Be still, and know that I am God."[8] As hard as it was, I knew I had to quit striving and trying to make things work my way. But rather, I had to let God do things his way and in his timing. I just hoped the time had finally come.

I knew Christopher would have to hit rock bottom before turning around. I had hoped his dismissal in 1994 would serve that purpose. Later, I had hoped his breakup with Kevin would be the turning point. Now I hoped that this situation—the threat not just of dismissal but expulsion—would be the catalyst that would cause Christopher to surrender his life to Christ. I didn't want things to get any worse.

At last Dr. Robinson's secretary said we could go into his office. Dr. Robinson was dean of the dental school, Dr. Johnson's superior. He met us at the door and greeted us with a cordial smile and handshakes. "Dr. Yuan, Mrs. Yuan," he said, "it's a pleasure to see you again." He nodded at Christopher and shook his hand too. "Chris."

Dr. Robinson was a gracious and dignified man. The situation could have been very uncomfortable, but he was polite and civil. Still, there was tension in the air. The last thing the dean needed was a lawsuit against the school.

He invited the three of us to take a seat, and he sat down behind his desk. "Dr. Yuan, Mrs. Yuan," he said, "as you know, Christopher is an adult. And it is unorthodox, indeed, for me to meet with the parents of an adult student to talk about his academic situation." He tapped a pencil on the edge of his desk. "But since Christopher has given us written permission, I'm sure we can find a way to talk through this respectfully and productively."[9]

"Yes," Leon agreed. "And I really appreciate you taking the time to meet with us."

I spoke up then. "Dr. Robinson, it's a very serious thing to expel a student only a few months before he graduates with a doctoral degree that has taken him six years to earn—two years at Loyola, two years here, and then repeating another two years as a result of his dismissal."

Dr. Robinson said, "Yes, Mrs. Yuan, I realize that, but—"

Leon chimed in. "Dr. Robinson, I know you are aware that Christopher has incurred huge student loans for his past four years as a student. Without a professional degree, he will have no means to pay back the loans."

Dr. Robinson opened his mouth to speak, but I continued. "Dr. Robinson, I have prayed long and hard over the last few days, and I think it's important that neither Leon nor I get in the way of what God might do in Christopher's life."

Dr. Robinson gave us a puzzled look and seemed not to understand what I had just said. Christopher was glancing nervously between Leon, me, and the dean.

"What I'm saying, Dr. Robinson, is that we should not try to influence the school's decision one way or the other. We know that you and your administration would not make a hasty decision, and that you would look over all the information and do whatever you think is right.

Christopher hasn't told us all the details of why the school is expelling him, but we trust your administration will make the correct decision."

Dr. Robinson was uncertain of what to say. There was a pause, and I continued. "I'm sure that few parents have met with you who didn't try to influence the school's decision. But we want to do what is right for Christopher." I took a deep breath. "Actually, it's not important that Christopher becomes a dentist. What's important is that Christopher becomes a Christ follower. Leon and I have flown down to Louisville to tell you"—I looked over at Leon—"that we will support whatever decision you make. I only pray that my son will turn to God."

Dr. Robinson just looked at us. He was speechless. Christopher's face began to turn red. Anger painted his eyes as he gripped the armrests on his chair.

Although my heart was breaking over Christopher's renewed anger toward us, I was at peace that we were not getting in God's way and enabling our son. Instead, we expressed our position and gave witness to the priority of a life surrendered to God above all else—even one's career. As a mother, I didn't want my son to experience pain or difficulty. But God's ways are not my ways, and sometimes letting a child face the consequences of his own actions is the only way to show true love.[10] In fact, just that morning I'd read Proverbs 3:12: "The LORD disciplines those he loves."

We walked through the office doors and took the elevator to the ground floor, where we exited into the bright March sunlight. Christopher walked in front of us, still fuming about what had just happened.

"Well," I looked at Leon, "I'm really glad that's over."

"Yeah, me too," he answered, squeezing my hand. "I just hope that this is it and that things don't get any worse."

Twelve

Circuit Parties

Christopher: April 7, 1996

Ed Dollwet tapped me on the shoulder and shouted in my ear, "Connie, meet Jordan!" I could hardly hear Ed over the pounding music and the buzz of twenty thousand men on the dance floor. It was Easter weekend, and we were at the White Party, one of the biggest, most glamorous parties on the circuit. This one was held at the Wyndham Hotel and Convention Center in Palm Springs.

I turned around and was struck speechless. Jordan was a tall, blond, Marlboro Man sort of guy. I had seen his face many times before in magazine photos and movies. His face—and more—was already familiar to me. I shook his hand. "You're Tom R——." I called him by the stage name he was using in his movies.

He flashed a perfect smile. "That's right," he said. "But to my friends, I'm Jordan."

"I'm Chris," I replied. "Ed likes to call me Connie."

"Well, if you're a friend of Ed's, then you're my friend too."

In the world of gay pornography, Tom was a superstar. A couple of years earlier, he had received the equivalent of an Oscar in the porn industry. He and many other men in this crowd were easily recognizable. Everywhere I looked, I saw models and actors, and they were not just from the pornography industry. There were people from the covers of major magazines, from movies and television shows. I was surrounded by beautiful people. And now I was being introduced to one of the most famous of all. I was absolutely dumbfounded.

I couldn't believe that this little Chinese kid—who had been ridiculed and mocked in grade school—was rubbing elbows with superstars. Getting kicked out of dental school had freed me up to focus on circuit parties and drug dealing with renewed energy. I was beginning to fit in as a personality on the circuit scene. I was outgoing and funny. But more important, people knew I had good drugs. I was selling to the hottest of the hot.

Jordan and I had an incredible weekend together. We danced and laughed and told everybody that we were long-lost twins, separated at birth. Jordan wasn't interested in me as anything more than a friend, and I was content to be his party buddy. So I was surprised when he called me on Tuesday morning after I returned to Louisville. "I had a great time in Palm Springs," he said.

"Me too. The party was great. One of the best ever."

"Listen," Jordan continued. "I was wondering if you'd like to come see me in San Francisco. I've got frequent-flyer miles, so you don't have to pay a thing."

I knew it was the Tuesday blues talking. Jordan and I had spent the long weekend on Ecstasy, and coming down off that high on Monday and Tuesday was jarring. Once the dopamine quits surging through your brain, you come down hard. Many people end up depressed—even suicidal—after partying all weekend. It's hard to be alone with the Tuesday blues.

"Sure," I said. "I'd love to."

Jordan picked me up at San Francisco International Airport that Friday, and after dropping my luggage off at his house we decided to go for a ride on his motorcycle. Jordan was a tall, strong, masculine guy. He let me borrow a pair of his leather riding chaps; they were too big, but I turned up the cuffs and tightened the belt. Then I climbed onto his bike and we rode along the Pacific Coast Highway. We stopped at the Chart House, a beautiful restaurant overlooking the ocean in Montara State Beach. The sun was warm, the sky was blue, and the ocean sparkled on the horizon.

We walked into the restaurant, helmets in hand, and waited at the hostess stand for a table. A few waiters who weren't busy noticed our gear.

"You guys comin' in from a ride?"

"Yep, that's right," Jordan said.

"What kind of bike ya' got?" the waiter asked.

"A Harley," Jordan said. "Fat Boy."

"Nice." The waiter nodded. "I just bought a Sportster 1200. Brand-new." He turned to me. "How about you? What do you ride?"

"Oh," I said, as a smile came across my face. "We rode together."

The waiter looked at me, then at Jordan, and then down at our leather chaps. "Oh…sure…right on." Jordan and I laughed as he and the other waiters walked awkwardly away. Gay couples weren't a novelty in San Francisco, but we didn't fit the stereotype. Plus, we were just friends. Jordan was lonely after the craziness of the weekend, and I was there to cheer him up.

We had a delicious lobster dinner as we watched the sun set over the Pacific. I offered to pay my part of the tab, but Jordan insisted, saying he'd invited me to come. *That's strange,* I thought. As he handed his credit card to the waitress, we made eye contact. For a brief moment, I saw something in his look that quickened my pulse. Was he interested in more than just friendship?

After a late night at the clubs, we slept late the following morning. Waking up in Jordan's bed, I had to pinch myself to make sure I wasn't dreaming. Could this be real?

Three weeks later, Jordan flew to Louisville for the weekend. It was the weekend of the Kentucky Derby, and that meant huge parties in the gay community as well as in the straight. I was already very popular in the

Louisville clubs, but having a famous star with me made me that much more visible. Together, Jordan and I sold a good amount of drugs, and we split the profits.

From Louisville, Jordan left for Chicago, where he was scheduled to make a paid appearance at a gay club. A few days later he called me from the Cook County Hospital.

"Chris, I'm sick," he said in a weak and raspy voice. He coughed, and I could hear the congestion deep in his chest. "I'm real sick…if you can't tell. I'm in the hospital."

Jordan had told me he was HIV positive on our first night together in San Francisco, but he had kept it a secret from the public.

"Is it HIV-related?" I asked.

"Yeah. They think it's pneumonia." He coughed again and couldn't stop for a few moments.

It was hard to imagine the big, strong man who'd partied with me just weeks earlier now laid up in a hospital with pneumonia.

Without much thought, I jumped in my car and left for Chicago. As soon as I entered the lobby of Cook County Hospital, I was hit by a terrible smell. It wasn't the usual disinfectant smell of a hospital; it had another smell I wasn't used to…the unmistakable stench of urine.

When I got to Jordan's room, the nurses told me he was quarantined. They made me put on a mask and gown just to enter his room. And when I saw him, it was worse than I had imagined. He had lost ten pounds in one week, and his face was gaunt. A few days earlier, people had thronged around him, eager to be near this gay icon. But now he was alone. Cook County Hospital wasn't where the rich and famous went when they got sick. It was the catchall hospital, where people in desperate need ended up.

I was the only one who came to see Jordan. None of his friends from the parties, no co-workers from the porn industry, no family came to see him. If I hadn't driven up from Louisville, Jordan would have spent the rest of the night alone in a cold, dark hospital room. Despite all his superstar status, no one but I came to be with him.

— — —

As Jordan slept fitfully through the night, I looked out the window at the city that used to be my home. I'd been here for a couple of days now, and I convinced myself that I'd feel guilty if I didn't at least tell my mom I was in town. The truth, though, was that I was lonely. To see a big star like Tom R—— wasting away to a skeleton scared me, and I wanted the comforting presence of a familiar person. So despite everything inside me that said no, I picked up the phone and called my parents.

They were excited to hear from me and immediately volunteered to come to the hospital. Even though I had wanted their company, I wasn't sure how I felt about this. I was afraid of what might come out of their mouths when they spoke with Jordan, who I'm sure they thought was the "enemy." Mom could be forceful in expressing her opinions, and even though Jordan had made great improvements with the antibiotics going through his system, he was still at his most vulnerable. I almost told them not to come, but before I knew it, the phone call ended and they were on their way.

Jordan was slowly making his way down the hospital corridor, and I stood next to him pulling his IV drip bag on a stand with wheels. We turned a corner near the nurses' station, and I saw my parents entering through wide double doors at the far end of the hall. My stomach tightened.

"My parents are here," I said.

He looked in their direction, then back at me. "Let's go on back to the room," he said. "I'd like to meet them."

Dad and Mom gowned up and put on sterile masks, just as I had done. I nervously glanced back and forth between them as they entered Jordan's room. But my anxiety let up when Mom made eye contact with Jordan. Her eyes, just peeping over the surgical mask, were full of compassion and love. She and Dad came and gave me a big hug, then crossed the room to Jordan's bed, leaned over and gave him a hug as well.

My parents sat beside Jordan's hospital bed for half an hour, talking, laughing, and carrying on with both of us. We didn't cover any major topics; we just talked like four old friends. I was shocked by the acceptance and compassion my parents showed me—and especially Jordan. All I could think of, sitting in that cramped hospital room, was that for all Jordan's fans and party friends, the two people sitting at his bedside in this hour of need were strangers—my parents. They stayed with him when he needed it the most.

Jordan survived that illness. Our dating relationship, however, didn't—though we remained friends. Meanwhile, I was getting itchy to leave Louisville, which was starting to seem passé now that I was traveling the country and partying with A-list people. The friends I had in Louisville just couldn't keep up with the fast-paced, jet-setting schedule I was keeping. So when I wasn't off to a spectacular circuit party, I'd drive to Atlanta to hit the clubs for the weekend.

— — —

It was another hot weekend in the middle of August, and although the 1996 Summer Olympics had just finished in Atlanta, the city was still buzzing with energy and excitement. I was there again for Hotlanta—a year after I met Ed Dollwet. It was Sunday night, and I was at the Heretic, a leather bar, where I met a guy named Derek. He was a stocky guy with a sandy brown goatee—a real man's man. We hit it off immediately.

Derek took me to his apartment, and I stayed the night. In the morning as he was making breakfast, I told him, "You know, I've been thinking about moving to Atlanta."

"Moving?" he said. "Where would you move to?"

"Oh, I don't know yet. You know my friends Chad and Jeff just moved here from Nashville. They've got a house off Ponce de Leon. Maybe I can move in with them."

"Well, what do you think of my place?" he asked, as he put scrambled eggs on a plate and turned to look at me.

"Sure," I said. "It's a great part of town. Much better than my place in Louisville."

"Then why don't you move in with me?"

"Really?" I asked. "Are you serious?"

"Yeah, I'm serious. Move in with me and Fletcher." Fletcher was his bull terrier.

"Well...all my stuff is in Louisville."

"Then let's get it. I'll go with you—this weekend—and help you move down here."

That weekend, Derek, Fletcher, and I drove to Louisville in a U-Haul van to pack up my stuff so I could move to Atlanta. It was my twenty-sixth birthday and the beginning of an exciting chapter of my life. But as we were driving through the rolling hills of Tennessee, my cell phone rang. It was Luke from L.A., Ed Dollwet's ex-boyfriend.

"Chris, I have some bad news," Luke said, his voice cracking. "Ed died yesterday."

I pushed the Off button, and my hand fell to my lap. Derek asked what was wrong, but I couldn't speak for a few moments. My mind was reeling, replaying scene after scene of Ed—in a club, on the phone, at a party, introducing me to Jordan and countless others. Suddenly, I had no one to call me Crazy Connie anymore. No one to look to for business advice. Mr. Ed had initiated me into the world I ran in—the drugs, the parties, the life. He was the first person I knew personally to die of AIDS, and the shock of losing him ran deep. It was a terrible blow on what otherwise would have been one of the happiest days of my life.

— — —

Life with Derek was a roller-coaster ride from the start. For the first few weeks, every morning he'd tell me how much he loved me, how glad he was I'd moved in with him. I felt like we had become one—our souls enmeshed. But in reality, much of the passion between us was fueled by Ecstasy—thus our relationship was fierce and intense, both good and bad.

Early in October, Derek wanted to go out on a Sunday night, but I didn't. He got dressed and went out anyway. I waited all night for him to return home, and he never came back—until morning. When I asked where he'd been, he got angry and told me that I should get my own place. So I started packing my stuff. I grabbed a framed picture of the two of us together, and he stormed up and grabbed it, saying, "That's mine."

I wouldn't let go, so he put me in a choke hold. Sure, we'd had our differences, but we'd never gotten into a physical fight with each other. As I gasped for air, I was in shock that this man, whom I loved, was doing this to me. Derek had told me so many times that I was the one. Now I couldn't break free of his strong grip, and he was about to kill me. Finally, he lowered me back to the floor and let go of my neck. As my feet touched the floor, he pushed me away and yelled, "Get out!" I grabbed my stuff and walked out the door as tears welled up in my eyes.

I should have been angry and upset with Derek, but I wasn't over him. He had almost strangled me, but still I was in love with him. Over the next few months, we tried to get back together. Once at his place, after I had stayed the night, he told me things from his past that I hadn't heard before. It wasn't easy for him to share his secrets, and I was glad he was opening up. Then he paused, and his shoulders dropped as he broke down. As we sat on the floor, tears rolled down his cheeks. He looked me in the eyes and told me he was HIV positive. He'd been afraid to tell me, he said. Afraid I wouldn't love him and afraid I would leave him.

Watching him cry, I reached out to him and forgave him for things he'd never even apologized for. As the implications of his confession dawned on me, I realized I wasn't angry—I actually felt sorry for him. It was bad enough that he was HIV positive; now he had to live with the fact that he might have infected me. I leaned over and put my arms around him.

"It's okay," I said. "It's okay."

I had been sexually involved with a man who was infected with the virus that caused AIDS, and he hadn't told me until just then. But strangely, I felt a sense of freedom. No longer did I have to wonder if I'd been infected. There was no need to get tested; it wouldn't make a difference anyway. Now I could live my life without worrying if I'd catch it. Now I was all in.

As we cried together, I felt that now I shared something intimate with Derek. In fact, I felt that I had attained something special in the gay community. I was part of the inner circle. Now I was one of them. I actually felt a little comforted by it all. Men who were HIV positive were lionized. They were profiled in gay magazines. They got their names put on quilts. Certainly, AIDS was a terrible thing; but I felt, somehow, that I'd become a hero.

Thirteen

Secret Shame

Angela: January 20, 1997

I t was Monday, the day I always fasted. Three and a half years had passed since I returned home from the turning-point trip to Louisville. Since then, I had committed myself to a water-only fast every Monday as I interceded for Christopher. But this day I was also fasting for my father, who had come to visit us the week before. I knelt in my prayer closet, holding a picture of my dad. He was a hard-working man, full of integrity and responsibility. He was known to be serious, harsh, strict, and most of all, very stubborn.

But after eighty-three years of hard living and fighting to fend for himself, he surrendered his life to Christ. It was a moment I wish I could capture forever. He actually knelt on our living room floor and prayed the sinner's prayer. And then he gave me a hug—the first and only hug I ever received from my father. I had never seen him cry before, but on that day he was crying and told me that his tears were not of sorrow but of joy.

Now if only my mom would be so open. They had been separated for more than three years. Before that, when they did live together, they stayed in different rooms and could barely stand to be with each other. There were so many things from the past that they hadn't dealt with, and they became more and more bitter toward each other over the years.

When I was growing up, the last thing I wanted was for my parents to be divorced. And that was why I had promised myself never to tell my dad a certain dark secret that I knew about my mom.

— — —

I was a small girl, around five years old, with dark hair that hung to my shoulders in sleek, shiny pigtails. I was a cute and chubby child, and my pajamas hung loosely from my body as I tossed in bed that night. My dad, a merchant marine, was away at sea, and I shared a bed with my mom—not an unusual thing for Chinese children. Suddenly my eyes snapped open. Something was not right.

I tried to make sense of the rocking motion I felt. *Knock. Knock. Knock. Knock.* The wooden headboard cracked against the wall, and as I rolled over I saw a dark form crouching over my mother. I heard the sighs and groans, and bile from my stomach rose into my chest. I let out a scream that pierced the night air—and still echoes in my mind today. Then I kicked so hard that the bed toppled and sheets were thrown across the room. In the moonlight, I saw Mr. Lee, a man I recognized from my mom's office. He suddenly jumped up, naked and clutching a pair of pants to his crotch. My mom took him out of the room, glaring at me over her shoulder.

I sat in bed with my knees pulled up to my chest and cried and cried and cried. I called out for my daddy, but he wasn't there. He was thousands of miles away, on the inky black ocean. No one came to comfort me. No one came to tell me that everything was going to be okay. I sat there choking on my tears as my little chest shook.

I felt frightened, ashamed, and most of all, dirty. I tried to forget that this ever happened, but I couldn't. The image of my mom's body entangled with that other man's played over and over in my head. It was a dark secret that would stay tucked away in the recesses of my mind, hidden from the rest of the world and hidden from my dad.

The following morning, in the dim light of the dawning sun, I wandered into the fields behind our house. I didn't know where my mother had gone, and she didn't come looking for me. I dropped to my knees in the mud and started digging. I pressed my small, bare fingers through the matted grass into the wet soil. I probed beneath the ground until my fingers found something solid: a bulbous root. I ripped it from its place in the ground and held it in my trembling hand as tears flowed down my face. The root was crusted with soil, but its white flesh showed through between the clumps of dirt.

As the image of my mom making love to a stranger ran through my head, my chest continued to shake from the lingering sobs. I grasped the root in my grubby fingers, held it to my teeth, and sucked on it. The grit of the soil, the succulence of the root, and the sweetness of the green grass mixed in my mouth. I sucked away the juice until a pasty grass pulp was left on my tongue. I spat the pulp into my hand and buried it back in the ground—just as I was going to bury this nightmare of a secret. I wanted so much to leave that nightmare buried deep in the reddish brown soil of Shanghai—never to be seen again. Then I grabbed another clump of grass, sucked, spit, and buried, repeating the process over and over. How else could a five-year-old girl handle such a repugnant horror?

I had tried to escape the ugly truth about my mother, but how could I when each day men continued to come through our home? They would arrive to "visit" with my mother during the long weeks when my dad was away on a merchant ship. I wanted to vomit. She insisted I call them "Uncle," but I refused. I wanted to spit in their faces, but instead I gave them looks of disgust and loathing. This infuriated my mother, and many times I ran out of the house and returned to that field, my fingernails black, my hands dirty and raw from digging. There was so much buried in my memory, so much covered in darkness. And those images—which no little girl should ever have to endure—soiled my childhood innocence and crippled my mind, heart, and soul.

— — —

Holding a secret for so many years affected my relationship with my parents, with Leon, and with my children. But fortunately now, with God's help, I had a way to deal with the past. During my days of fasting, I was able to lay my secrets and burdens before God and begin the process of healing.

I could understand the agony that Christopher went through as a young boy when he kept his deep dark secret of homosexuality from everybody else. I knew why he felt that no one could understand him and his pain. I could understand the shame and guilt that he endured, even though none of it was his fault. No wonder it was so freeing for him to finally "come out." I only wished that he would take all his burdens and issues and surrender them to Christ. I wanted him to know that his family loved him—and that God loved him even more. But I knew that Leon and I—as much as we loved our son—faced competition from Christopher's gay friends.

I imagined Christopher like a little boy on a school playground with other children. I'd try to get his attention, but he would ignore me. I would try to get him to come home, but he wouldn't leave his friends. I knew that Christopher was so attached to his friends that he considered them his real family. And I prayed that somehow he would see the priority of not only a relationship with his family but also—more important— a relationship with God.

A couple of years earlier, I had decided to send him cards several times a week so that he would know we still thought about him and hadn't forgotten him. *If he won't answer our phone calls,* I thought, *he can still receive cards.* I figured I could at least plant seeds. So I would buy a stack of Christian greeting cards, and during my prayer times, I would often write a note to Christopher, telling him that I had been praying for him. Sometimes I would share a passage of Scripture that meant something to me. And at the bottom of each card, I signed it, *Love you forever, Mom.*

I wanted to be the extension of God's love to Christopher, and I wanted him to know that our door would always be open to him, no matter what he did or what might happen. God was planting deep roots in my life—roots that would hold firm in the hardest trials. I didn't know what was next for Christopher, but I had a feeling that things were not going to get better anytime soon.

Fourteen

The High Life

Christopher: Spring 1997

"Thirty minutes until show time!" I called out over the music playing through my stereo. It was about five thirty on a Saturday evening, and my friends Jack, Billy, and Mack were helping me get ready for "office hours."

I had begun to limit drug sales to certain days and times, Friday and Saturday evenings from six to ten o'clock. Before this, people had been coming to my apartment to buy drugs at any time of the day or night. So I announced a new policy: if you want to get your drugs before you go to the clubs, you need to come during my office hours.

"Hey, Billy, how many quarter bags of ice we got?" Sitting in my bedroom, Billy was busy using a digital scale, weighing out quarter grams of crystal meth and putting them into blue, one-inch square, zip-top baggies. "We'll need at least a hundred for the next few hours and another hundred for the clubs."

"Yeah, we're doing good, Chris," Billy called back. "We've got a hundred in the safe, and I've got just about a hundred right here."

Jack was in a walk-in closet, using an electric coffee grinder to break up a brick of cocaine. The grinder was perfect for making it nice and fluffy. "Make sure you grind it good, Jack. Someone said the coke was a little chunky last week."

"Got it. Customer satisfaction is our number-one priority! A happy customer is a repeat customer!" Jack had a way of making us laugh. And just then we began singing as Abba's "Dancing Queen" started to play through my speakers.

I walked past Jack and opened my fireproof safe. In it were several nylon, color-coded bags. Blue was where I stored baggies of ice. Green was for cocaine. Purple was for Ecstasy. Red was the bulkiest bag because it was full of small glass vials with my own special, cherry-flavored ketamine, or special K. White was the catchall bag for everything else: Valium, acid, steroids, and so on.

Mack was straightening out my apartment and brought me a stack of mail. "Hey, Connie, what should I do with these? I think they're mostly bills."

"Put them in that desk tray organizer." I pointed to the corner of my desk. "Walter comes on Tuesdays to pay my bills, and he'll take care of all that."

"Oh wait, what's this?" Mack asked as he pulled out a bright-colored envelope. "Look, it's another card from your mom. Aww, that's so sweet."

"Yeah, more Christian propaganda." I ripped it open to see if she had sent anything extra. "No money. You know where I put her cards. Throw it in her file," I said, as I pointed to the garbage. He tossed the card into the trash.

The doorbell rang, and I checked my watch. "Unbelievable. It's not even six yet and they're banging on the door. Mack, can you grab that? And tell them to wait a few minutes." I pulled envelopes full of cash from the safe to make sure we had enough tens and twenties for change.

"Chris, it's Kyle," Mack said. "He says he had an appointment. Should I let him in?"

"Oh yeah! Let him in."

Kyle was a local dealer. The people who could show up outside established office hours were those who bought in bulk—and made an appointment. He walked into the living room, looking frazzled, strung out, and skinnier than last week. He was already thin, but on this night he looked like a bag of bones.

"Hey, Kyle," I patted him on the back. "Man, you need to be taking better care of yourself. Don't forget to eat!"

"Yeah, I'm sorry, Chris. I'm…I'm s-s-sorry that I'm late. I couldn't find my keys and…um…it took me…um…about an hour to find my keys, and…and th-then while I was driving here…um…somehow I got lost."

Lost? I thought. *You've driven here a hundred times.*

"We'll, I guess you're here now. How much do you want?"

"Can I get two ounces of t-tina?" he asked, requesting the one thing I was best known for selling—high-quality crystal methamphetamine. His eyes seemed to get bigger when he said "tina," and his pupils were already so big I felt like I could jump into them.

"Let's see," I said, as I looked through my records. "Last time I gave you a really good deal. And since I'm such a nice guy, I'm going to stick to that. Two ounces, that's $3,200."

"Oh, great." Kyle fumbled through his backpack to pull out a thick envelope.

"Those are big bills, right?" I said.

"Yeah, of course. And they are all…um…all neat and folded, and neatly folded, and f-f-facing the same way, j-just like how you like 'em. I even ironed… I-I ironed the bills just to get them j-just the way you like 'em." His hands shook as he passed three wrapped stacks of one-hundred-dollar bills to me, along with two loose bills. I took the three stacks over to my digital scale, removed the paper money wrap, and put each stack on the scale, measuring the weight of the bills to the milligram.

"Great, it looks like we've got exactly $3,200 here. Mack, can you put this money in my safe and get out two ounces of tina for our friend Kyle?"

Kyle took the two bags of ice, which were about the size of his hand, and stuffed them into his backpack. As he walked out the door, he almost tripped on the doorstep and knocked over my dry-erase board, which said, *Office Hours: 6 p.m. to 10 p.m.* He passed people who were lined up outside my door. "Is he open?" someone said.

"I h-h-had an appointment," we heard Kyle stutter as the door closed behind him. I sighed and thought, *What a sketchy mess!* The four of us scrambled to get the last-minute details together.

"Hey, Billy, fix the pillows on my couch, and, Jack, can you light the candles? Oh, and crank up the music because we're now…open for business!" I threw open the door to see a line of people leading down two flights of steps to the bottom. Fortunately, most of my neighbors were young, single, gay, and partiers themselves—and many were my customers. I didn't know of any kids or families who lived around here. Besides, this was Midtown—the gay capital of Atlanta.

"Hey, everybody! Beautiful night, isn't it? Come on in, ten at a time."

There was friendly chatter as people walked in and found seats in my living room, waiting to order. Billy wrote the orders in his notebook, and then Mack brought customers into the bedroom where Jack and I were filling orders. We took turns counting the money and handing out drugs.

"Would you like paper or plastic?" Jack asked, then put a couple hits of Ecstasy into a little baggie. It was all so surreal, like a game to us.

As ten o'clock neared, people were still gathered outside. Billy began running in to fill the smaller orders. We were finally finished at eleven, and we started to get ready to go out to party. First we hit Blue, the happening gay club where everybody went—at least for that season. When it closed at four o'clock in the morning, we headed over to Backstreet, Atlanta's twenty-four-hour nightclub. Most people who weren't ready to call it a night after the bars closed ended up there.

As we pulled my new sports car into the parking lot, we noticed a long line stretching from the front door. We walked straight to the front, and security cleared the way, letting us in without making us wait or even pay the cover fee. Jack, Billy, Mack, and I took off our shirts and strapped blinking bicycle safety lights to our belts so partiers in need of drugs could find us in the dark. As we walked through the crowded front room, people tried to stop us, but I'd tell them, "Meet me on the dance floor." I was determined to get to the action and feel the beat of the music, surrounded by several hundred sweaty men.

When we got to the top of the stairs heading down into the main dance floor, you could see the sea of bodies drawn like a magnet toward us. Everybody saw our lights. We pushed our way down the steps, and standing next to one another on the dance floor, we began selling as people lined up to place their orders.

"What would you like?" I asked.

"Two hits of X and a gram of K. Do you have any cherry K?"

"Of course. That's $110. Do you have exact change? We prefer exact change."

"Yes, it's right here."

He stuffed the money into my hand, all crumpled up. I flattened it out to make sure it was the right amount, but it was difficult to see in the dark. So I lifted it in the air and waited for the disco lights to shine in my direction, then quickly counted the bills. All there. I pulled out my Tic Tac box.

"Give me your hand."

"Right here?"

"Yeah. They're just mints, right?" I said with a wink.

"Okay," he said, looking around. "What about my K?"

"Check your front pocket." I had already slipped the small vial of K into his pants. Surprised, he walked away.

"Hey, Greg," I called to the next guy. "How are you? Haven't seen you in a while. What can I do for you?"

Most nights my pockets were so stuffed with cash that I had to go out to my car just to empty them out. I was on top of the world—rich, popular, and powerful. It was more than anyone could dream of. *This must be what it's like to be God.*

— — —

Over time, I became less of a dealer and more of a supplier, which meant that I needed to be more creative in how I transported money and drugs. I received most of my shipments via a rented mailbox at a nearby private postal center. For sending shipments to my customers, FedEx was quick and simple. But sometimes if I needed an order delivered right away, I'd use air cargo delivery and stuff a videocassette recorder with drugs. It was quite a bit more expensive, but I could get things delivered on the same day.

For larger purchases, I would fly to a destination and sometimes bring along a friend. We would travel with money strapped to our bodies—less than ten thousand dollars on each person and in each bag, because we were afraid the metal strips in so many bills would set off a metal detector. And we'd come back with ice or Ecstasy stuffed in our socks and under-wear, strapped to our legs and bodies, or hidden in the lining of our luggage. Fortunately, plastic bags of drugs didn't set off metal detectors. The first few trips we made were nerve-racking. But after a while it was no big deal, and we actually got a rush out of doing it.

Now with access to larger quantities, I was supplying people in about a dozen states. I had everything I wanted—a nice apartment, a fancy car, designer clothes. So with a little more time and money on my hands due to being a supplier, I was looking for something else to do.

There wasn't much to do on Sunday afternoons in Atlanta's gay community. After the throbbing insanity of Friday and Saturday nights, the clubs closed at four o'clock on Sunday morning. People would either go to Backstreet for a couple more hours or go home. And for the most part, they still hadn't come down off the drugs from the previous night. Our only option was Fat Tuesday, a frozen daiquiri bar in ritzy Buckhead, north of Midtown. But there was no dance floor at Fat Tuesday. So my marketing mind kicked in as I remembered the Sunday afternoons at many circuit parties: the Sunday tea dance.

I thought it would be a great idea to have a regular, ongoing Sunday tea dance in Atlanta and use a straight dance club venue to add to the novelty. Why would anyone want to go back to the same gay club they'd been partying at Saturday night? I found a cool straight club in Buckhead called the Chili Pepper and made an appointment with the brothers who owned the place.

"How'd you like to make some extra money?" I asked them. "I can pack your club on a Sunday afternoon, when you would normally be closed—and with clientele who would not normally come to your bar." That got their attention. "Since you usually don't make anything on Sundays, let's make a deal. I get the money from the cover charge at the door, and I'll be responsible for all the promotions and the DJ. And you get all the money from the bar. You provide bartenders and security, and agree not to charge me any rent for the use of your club." It was an unorthodox proposal, but they accepted since it would be extra income.

I spared no expense. I flew in the best DJs from Miami, New York, Montreal. I paid professional graphic artists to design high-quality fliers and posters, which were printed out of state. We blanketed Midtown with my fliers, and word spread quickly.

CHRIS YUAN PRESENTS

ICE

A SUNDAY TEA DANCE

4 pm until Midnight
at the Chili Pepper
with DJ Mark Anthony
(Black & Blue, Montreal)

Ice. That was what I was known for. I had the best ice in town. All the money from the door was put back into the DJ, promotions, and incidental costs. I was basically throwing these parties at cost so I'd have another place to sell drugs. I didn't care who knew it. I sold lots of drugs at each event and became more and more of a local celebrity.

The biggest ice party was held after Hotlanta 1997. The club's capacity was a little more than two thousand people, but we had over three thousand crammed inside. Steam rose from the dance floor, where well-known DJ Mark Anthony, who headlined at the world's largest circuit party, was spinning. I could see that the club's balcony was flexing and swaying with the weight of hundreds of people who couldn't get on the main dance floor.

It was an incredible party, and it was my party, with my name on it: "Chris Yuan Presents." Old friends and new thronged around me. Whether they liked me or just my drugs didn't make much difference to me: I was the hottest thing in Atlanta on that day. Some of my old friends from Nashville came down for my tea dance, but they had to stand in line for half an hour just to say hello.

I felt like I was truly larger than life. This was it. Chris Yuan had arrived.

Fifteen

Lost

Angela: Summer 1997

It was seventy degrees and sunny. A few cotton-ball clouds floated slowly across the clear Atlanta sky. As nice as the weather was, it was hard to enjoy it on this day. Leon and I had been sitting on a bench at the arrivals area outside Hartsfield-Jackson Atlanta International Airport. After almost two hours, I was feeling dizzy from all the exhaust fumes. I had a headache from the rumbles, squeaks, and sighs of shuttle buses driving by. I looked down the long driveway leading up to the terminal with as much hopeful expectation as I could muster.

"I don't think he's coming," Leon said.

"Maybe he'll be here any minute."

Lord, give me love, joy, peace, patience...[11]

"What do you think has happened to him?" Leon asked, as he stood up and put a hand on his luggage.

"Maybe he got held up. Maybe there's construction on the road." I tried to come up with excuses for Christopher's tardiness.

Love bears all things, believes all things, hopes all things, endures all things.[12] I was trying not to give up hope, but it wasn't easy. I couldn't help thinking about all the times we wanted Christopher to come home and had even bought him plane tickets. But he'd call to cancel at the last minute—except this past Christmas.

— — —

It was late afternoon on Christmas Eve as I drove down Chicago's wintery streets to O'Hare Airport. Only a little dusting of snow covered the roads. *Good,* I thought. *Hopefully the flights won't be delayed.* For weeks leading up to this day, I'd been afraid that Christopher would cancel—just as he had done so many times before. But he didn't. Leon and I had called him the day before and left a message that I would meet him at the airport.

We had prepared his room for this visit. We planned to cook all his favorite dishes and invited family and friends to celebrate with us. If we'd had a fatted calf, we would've gladly killed it for Christopher's homecoming dinner.

I got to the airport early, just in case his plane was ahead of schedule. After parking the car, I walked into the terminal and looked on the monitors for the Atlanta flight. Arriving at the gate, I staked out a spot right at the opening of the jet bridge. The jet pulled up to the gate, and the excitement was almost more than I could stand. Passengers filed past me, hugging and kissing their loved ones with smiles, tears, and laughter. I stood on my toes and strained to see who was coming around the corner. Finally, a head of short, black hair was peeping over the shoulder of a taller man. I couldn't control my excitement—I jumped and moved forward to greet him. But then I stopped. It wasn't Christopher.

"Sorry," I mumbled, and the Asian man glanced in my direction and scooted out of my way. I stepped back, embarrassed, but continued to look down the jet bridge at still more passengers exiting the plane. About ten minutes passed, and the flow of people slowed to a trickle. Finally, the last people walked by me—the flight attendants and pilots. But no Christopher.

I took in a deep breath. *Maybe he just missed his flight. Maybe he'll be on the next flight from Atlanta.* I walked to the nearby monitor to see if any more planes were coming that day from Atlanta. There was one more flight later that evening. So I went home and returned three hours later to the airport.

I found the gate and again stood at the opening of the jet bridge. "Delta Flight 1612 arriving at gate E12," a voice announced over the loudspeaker.

The people around me immediately started chattering. A young woman placed her small child on her hip, a college-age man held a small bouquet of flowers, an elderly couple slowly moved to where they could see better, and a lady off to my right raised a handmade sign that said *Welcome Home.*

Once again positioned at the front of the crowd, I peered down the jet bridge, anxious to catch a glimpse of my son. I held my breath as people began to head up the passageway toward us. As they approached, their weariness from traveling was replaced with eager anticipation. A father dropped his suitcase at the side of the door just in time to catch the racing embrace of his young, pigtailed daughter. As happiness surrounded me, I couldn't help but feel pangs of jealousy. One by one, passengers were welcomed into the arms of their loved ones. Slowly, the people who had waited at the gate found the ones they had been waiting for and walked away.

All except me. I stood there alone, with no one I could welcome home. Countless faces had filed past me—all unrecognizable, all strangers— and not one of those faces matched that of my precious son. I stood looking down the hallway—now empty—and finally had to face the reality that Christopher was not coming home for Christmas.

I felt like dropping to my knees on the hard, concrete floor. My eyes welled up with tears. I couldn't hold them back any longer. The pain I felt was the same as if I had lost my son...all over again.

— — —

Now, several months later, I was waiting once again—but at a different airport. On a bench outside the Atlanta airport terminal, I fought the same sinking feeling. For more than two hours, Leon and I had been stranded. We'd decided after Christmas that if Christopher wouldn't come home, then we would go visit him. But now that we were in Atlanta, there still wasn't any sign of our son.

"Let me try calling him one more time," I said.

"All right," Leon answered, shifting on the hard bench and glancing again at his watch.

I could tell he was fighting frustration, so I gave him a reassuring smile and patted his shoulder. Then I headed to the pay phone for the fourth time. The call went directly in to Christopher's voice mail. I simply shook my head as I sat down again at Leon's side. He took in a deep breath.

"Well," he said, "let's get a taxi."

I glanced at my watch. "How about another fifteen minutes? He must be lost."

"Lost?" Leon said. "Yes, Christopher is certainly lost—in more ways than one."

But instead of hailing a cab, we continued to wait. And after we had spent three hours on the hard bench, Christopher finally arrived. He pulled up in a sleek, metallic-silver 1997 Honda Prelude. *How on earth could he afford such a car?* I wondered. *Does he have a job now?*

"Hey, M-Mom. Hey, Da-ad," Christopher said, acting as if nothing was wrong. He walked over and gave us a short, stiff hug. Although he was polite, there was no warmth in his greeting. He was wearing tight, cutoff jeans, a tank top, and boots. His face was greasy, and he had dark bags under his eyes. He was so skinny—nothing but skin and bones. Christopher seemed distracted as he looked around and walked first to the front of the car, then back and around again to the side. Finally, he opened the trunk so we could put our bags in.

He's acting so strange, I thought. *I wonder what's wrong.*

I crawled into the backseat of his little two-door car, and Leon sat in the passenger seat next to Christopher.

"Okay, ready to…um…okay, l-let's go," Christopher said, as the car lurched forward. He mumbled something to himself as he nervously checked the rearview and side mirrors. As we merged onto Interstate 85 north, Christopher weaved a bit in and out of traffic. It was my first time in Atlanta, but it seemed that we drove past the downtown area. And Christopher continued driving. *Strange,* I thought, since I knew he lived not too far from downtown.

Then Christopher pulled off the interstate. He turned left off the exit ramp, crossed over the interstate, then got back on the highway headed in the opposite direction. I could see Christopher's furrowed eyebrows in the rearview mirror. He looked puzzled and disoriented. After a few miles, he got off at another exit ramp and was about to turn left. Then he changed his mind and made a right turn. He drove several miles in one direction, then turned around and drove several miles the way we had just come.

Next, he left the main road and drove slowly on twisting roads in small neighborhoods until we came to a business district. He pulled into a gas station and rolled down his window.

"Ex-excuse me, s-sir," Christopher asked a man pumping gas into his car. "Um, d-d-do I turn right or left, um, or right on Peach-ch-tree?" He could barely get the words out.

The man looked at him, puzzled. "This is not Peachtree. What road are you looking for, son?"

"I know this is P-Peachtree!" Christopher said, sounding angry.

"Where are you going?" the man asked again.

"F-forget it…stu-stupid people…" Christopher stepped on the gas and pulled out of the station, catching the curb as we rolled back onto the street.

Where is he going? I thought. *Doesn't he know how to get to his own home?* Leon was as perplexed as I was.

Christopher drove us around Atlanta for close to two hours, trying to find his way home. We wanted to spend all our time with Christopher, but he'd told us in advance that he had plans on this Saturday night. So, with no other choice, we had arranged to have dinner with Jim and Joyce, friends who lived in Dacula. We would also stay the night with them. By the time we got back to Christopher's apartment, they were already on their way to pick us up.

"Christopher, tomorrow's Sunday. Would you like to come to church with us?" I asked. "We plan to go to a church called First Baptist Church Atlanta. We can give you the address so you can meet us there, if you want." Dr. Charles Stanley was a well-known preacher, and I thought if Christopher could hear one of his messages, maybe it would be a turning point for him.

"Yeah, wh-whatever," he said, rifling through a stack of papers on the kitchen counter, trying to look busy. We were writing the church's address for him when the phone rang; Jim and Joyce were calling to let us know they were outside.

Leon and I walked to the front door. "Okay, we're leaving now. Bye. Love you…" We pulled our luggage out the door. Christopher didn't even bother to look up.

— — —

On Sunday morning, Leon and I arrived early at First Baptist so we could reserve a seat for Christopher. We had tried calling him earlier that morning, but there was no answer. Leon looked around the foyer full of people but couldn't find our son. We grabbed a seat in a place where I could easily see the entrances to the sanctuary—in case Christopher showed up. The service started and the songs of praise began to calm my spirit. I kept looking over my shoulder to see if Christopher was at the doors, but he was nowhere in sight.

As they were about to sing the last song, I scanned the faces in the back but did not see Christopher. Voices from the sanctuary began to sing, "God will make a way, where there seems to be no way."[13] I grabbed Leon's hand as I recognized the familiar words. Leon squeezed my hand in return. This song held deep meaning for both of us.

If I had ever needed God to make a way, it was now. Christopher seemed more and more hopeless, more and more unreachable. Everything we did to express our love and show an interest in his life seemed to fail. It seemed that there was no way of getting through to him—and this day was no exception. My heart ached as I continued to look toward the entrances to the church sanctuary. Nothing. No Christopher. As Dr. Stanley began his message and continued for a few minutes, I quit looking back at the doorways.

Then an hour into the service, out of the corner of my eye, I spotted Christopher in the back. He stood leaning against a wall, sticking out like a sore thumb among people dressed in their Sunday best. I nudged Leon and whispered, "He's here!" I wanted to motion to him so he could see us. But before I knew it, he ducked back through an exit and disappeared.

Sixteen

High Church

Christopher: Summer 1997

I don't know how I was talked into showing up at church—and First Baptist Church Atlanta, of all places. I didn't even make it back to my apartment from a night out with friends; I headed straight to church from the club. I arrived late and stood in the back of a huge sanctuary, wondering, *How am I going to find my parents? Why did I even come here?*

But here I was, wearing the same clothes I'd partied in the night before. Not exactly your normal church attire—especially for this rather formal, traditional church. I laughed to myself as I put my hand in my pocket and touched the metal cigar case that held my glass pipe. *Well, I've still got some tina. Maybe this would be a good place to "crack on"!*

I slid out of the sanctuary and found the men's room. Locking the stall door, I sat on the toilet and was grateful that no one else was in the room. *They're all "worshiping" God,* I mocked. *Well, that's their opiate. I've got mine!*

I pulled out my pipe and poured a few shards of ice into the small opening of the glass bowl. I fumbled in my pocket for my butane torch lighter, pulled it out, and flipped off the cap. The high started even before I hit the pipe. I could taste it, smell it, feel it filling my lungs. My ears began to buzz, and my fingertips started to tingle. The anticipation and the chase were like hors d'oeuvre before a banquet.

I steadied my trembling hands as I clicked on the lighter and held the hissing blue flame just inches below the bowl of the glass pipe. I rhythmically waved the flame back and forth under the pipe as I had done hundreds of times before. As the shards of ice melted, I calmly let out all the air from my lungs through my nose.

Then the ice suddenly came to a boil, and I pulled the torch back a bit to keep the ice from burning. I slowly took in a deep, controlled breath—not too fast to cool off the boiling meth and not too slow to overheat and burn this precious liquid—just enough to allow every bit of steam to go up the glass pipe and through my mouth to fill my lungs.

I held my breath for as long as I could, and instantly the ringing began in my ears—like the persistent ringing after attending a loud rock concert. A tingling sensation swept over my entire body. I closed my eyes and grabbed hold of the side of the bathroom stall to steady myself. The head rush came like a bullet train boiling out of a tunnel. I exhaled, and a huge, thick billow of smoke filled the small bathroom stall.

Now, this is what I call worship.

Seventeen

A Bold and Dangerous Prayer

Angela: Summer 1997

As the closing hymn began, I murmured, "Jesus, speak to Christopher in your own miraculous way. Bring him to yourself and soften his hardened heart."

The music came to a close, and I looked around the sanctuary for Christopher. There he was, standing against the back wall, looking at his pager. Jim and Joyce had invited the three of us to join them for lunch, and Christopher agreed to come. But he was distracted the whole time at the restaurant, taking calls on his phone or getting up from the table to use the restroom—not once, not twice, but numerous times. Every time he came back, he seemed a little more agitated. It was obvious that he wanted to leave.

Christopher drove Leon and me back to his apartment. It didn't matter what topic I brought up, Christopher was short and argumentative with me. Leon and I felt like we were walking on eggshells. We didn't want to say anything that would upset him, so we spent the rest of the night at his apartment in silence. Christopher sat in his room with the door closed, making it clear that he wanted nothing to do with us.

- - -

Leon and I woke up early Monday morning after sleeping on Christopher's sofa bed. Since Christopher was going to be busy that night, he had suggested we stay with friends. So we had already made plans to stay with friends in Marietta, just north of Atlanta, and they wanted to have all three of us over for lunch at noon.

Nine o'clock came. Leon and I finished our prayers and morning devotions, but Christopher was still sleeping. Ten o'clock came. Still no sign of Christopher. Eleven o'clock. The door to his room was closed, and there was no sound coming from inside. Eleven thirty. Time to leave, and still nothing.

"What should we do?" I asked Leon.

"We have thirty minutes to get there," he said. "We should leave now if we're going to make it in time."

"Okay, I guess I'll go in and wake him up. He should be up by now anyway."

I walked down the hall and slowly opened the door to Christopher's bedroom. "Christopher?" I said softly. "It's eleven thirty... We need to leave soon to meet Dr. Wu and Karen for lunch... It's time to get up."

Christopher threw his sheets back and sat up in bed. "Get out!" he yelled, fixing a hateful stare on me. "Get out of my room!"

I backed away from his door and into the living area where Leon was waiting. Christopher was close behind me, cinching a bathrobe around his waist. "I want you out of my place. Now!" He glared at me. "I didn't ask you to come here."

"I'm sorry, Christopher. You don't have to go to lunch with us. But can you just drop us off at Dr. Wu's place?"

"No!" Christopher yelled. He looked at our luggage by the door. "You've already got your bags packed," he said. "Just get out!"

"How can we leave?" I asked. "We don't have a car."

"That's not my problem," he shouted. "Just get out!"

"Then let us call Dr. Wu so he can pick us up," Leon suggested.

"No!" Christopher screamed. "Get out!"

As I stood there in shock, Leon was reaching into his bag to pull something out. It was his Bible—the only Bible he had ever owned. "Christopher," he said calmly through the tension in the room. "There's something I want to give you before we go." He held it out to our son.

"Are you serious? I don't want your stupid Bible! I don't even want you to think that I might read it!" Christopher yelled. "I don't want your religion. I don't want your Bible. I don't want you here. Just leave! Get out! And if you ever, ever bring up God or the Bible, you will never see me again!"

With his back toward us, he stood waiting for us to leave. Leon looked at me and then left his Bible on Christopher's kitchen counter. We grabbed our bags and walked out the door. As I looked back, I saw Christopher pick up Leon's Bible and throw it into the trash. He then walked to the open front door and slammed it shut behind us.

— — —

When Leon and I got back home to Chicago, the reality of our disastrous visit set in. We were at a crossroads. If we headed in one direction, we'd travel down the road of despair. But the other direction was...hope. Everything pertaining to Christopher was pushing us toward despair. How could our son treat us with such disdain? How could he be so angry and unyielding? How could he act as if we were his enemies?

It may have just been easier for us to give up on our son, but God said, *Wait!* He gave us the faith to hope against all the evidence we saw and to trust that he had a plan. Leon and I committed to focus not on hopelessness but on the promises of God.

I had already asked friends from Bible Study Fellowship and church to pray for Christopher. In addition to our own prayers, we had more than one hundred prayer warriors interceding on Christopher's behalf. Ever since I'd come back from Louisville, I'd fasted every Monday for my son. But after our trip to Atlanta, I felt God was calling me to fast for a longer period of time. So I began a juice-only fast with no end in mind. It lasted thirty-nine days.

During that time I wrote down many prayers in my journal. There were a few that I would recite each morning and throughout the day. I was so afraid that God might somehow forget about my son! So like the persistent widow, I would repeat them relentlessly, asking God to act. Asking God to have mercy on Christopher. Asking for a miraculous breakthrough. I knew that it would take nothing short of a miracle to bring this prodigal son to the Father. This was one of those prayers:

> *I'll stand in the gap for Christopher. I'll stand until the victory is won, until Christopher's heart changes. I'll stand in the gap every day, and there I will fervently pray. And, Lord, just one favor, don't let me waver. If things get quite rough, which they may, I'll never give up on that son, nor will you. Though the Enemy seeks to destroy, I'll not quit as I intercede, though it may take years. I give you my fears and tears as I trust every moment I plead.*

I was afraid to ask too much of God. I just wanted to know that Christopher was his and that my son would be safe—if not in this life, then in eternity. I got down on my knees and asked God to please give me just one day—even one hour—of knowing that Christopher had received Christ before I died. That's all I dared to ask of him.

Eighteen

Busted

Christopher: January 27, 1998

I was getting out of the shower when the doorbell rang. I called out to Rick—a guy I'd met at a club over the weekend—who was in my bedroom, changing his clothes.

"Can you get the door?" I said. "I'll be right out."

I heard the click and squeak of the door opening, then the sound of unfamiliar voices. It wasn't the friendly chatter of friends or customers. I walked out of the bathroom with a towel around my waist and saw a dozen men in black uniforms standing in my apartment. Their caps read *DEA* and *Atlanta Police*. I felt the blood drain from my face.

I had just received a shipment of drugs, and the boxes lay open on my kitchen counter. There were several ounces of ice and about three hundred hits of Ecstasy right there in plain view. If ever there was "probable cause" for DEA agents to enter without a warrant, this was it. They pushed past my friend, who stood there speechless.

My heart sank into my stomach. They separated me from Rick, taking me back to my bedroom and keeping him on the living-room couch. They closed the bedroom door and began to question me. I insisted they let my friend go. I explained that I'd just met him over the weekend and he was not involved with the drugs. They didn't believe me at first, but I continued to plead with them. Eventually they took the rest of his clothes out to him and let him go. I was allowed to get dressed, then they brought me to the kitchen table and started asking me questions.

"Who do you get your drugs from?" an agent asked, putting his face just inches from mine. I felt like I was back in Marine Corps boot camp. "Tell us, where do you get your ice?"

I was trying to decide whether to talk or wait for a lawyer when an agent stuck his head out of my bedroom doorway.

"Boss, you need to come here and look at this—like now."

"Watch him," the one they called Boss said to another agent.

I had no idea what they had found. Could it be paraphernalia, drugs, money... I heard my filing cabinet close and another drawer being pulled open. *My business records!*

Out of habit from working in my dad's dental office, I kept all my receipts and recorded my major business transactions. It helped me remember whom I sold to or bought from, how much I sold or bought, and how much I charged or paid. I used code names for drugs and people, but I realized now that they wouldn't be too hard to decipher. Filed with the records were receipts and bills: phone bills, hotel receipts, plane-ticket stubs, credit-card statements—certainly a gold mine for any DEA agent.

They took me to the filing cabinet in my walk-in closet and asked, "Why in the world did you keep all your receipts? Did you think you were going to file income-tax returns?"

I shrugged and couldn't help but smile. "It's just how I was raised."

Suddenly Jack, a friend who had a key to my apartment, walked in the front door. "Hey, Chris—" He looked up and froze. Several agents rushed toward the front door while they pushed me down on my bed, shutting the door between us. I heard agents in the other room tell Jack to sit on the couch. Again, I told the agents to let my friend go, that Jack was my best friend, not a dealer or a supplier. I knew that these agents wanted to catch dealers and suppliers, not users. Earlier, they listened to me and let Rick go. Would they believe me again for Jack? For once, I was actually telling the truth. But they didn't seem very willing. I needed some leverage.

Then I heard my phone ring. *Great,* I thought. *Who's calling now?* I heard agents scrambling in the other room and someone said, "Don't worry, Boss. It's the fax machine."

I often received orders by fax, and the machine picked up automatically. I heard the high-pitched squeal of the transmission, and within moments I heard the machine spit out a piece of paper. My mind was racing, trying to figure out which of my customers or suppliers it could be, when an agent opened the door and walked in with a piece of paper.

"Boss, it looks like Sammy Long in L.A. just got Chris's payment for a pound of ice. And fortunately for us, he'll be shipping it today."

Boss looked at me and said, "This might be a good time for you to start talking."

I hadn't been drug free for a while, but this was the most sober I had felt in years. What were my options? I could just keep my mouth shut and protect my suppliers and my customers. They said they'd be there for me—always. But if I refused to talk, I ran the risk that the agents might take in my best friend, Jack, and still throw me in prison for a long, long time.

I had taken pride in the fact that I was a drug dealer who was professional and had an education, business experience, and a knack for problem solving. But now I couldn't even come up with any good options.

"Well?" Boss said as he looked at me.

"Okay…I'll help. But you need to let my friend go…please." Boss thought for a second, then signaled to an agent standing by the door. He opened the door and said, "Let him go."

"So, again… Who do you get your drugs from?" asked the agent standing above me.

"I get my stuff…um…from a guy up north… His name is Kareem

Abbas." *Yes,* I thought. *That's it.* Kareem had totally ripped me off a few months earlier when he gave me a couple thousand bad hits of Ecstasy, which cost me twenty-seven thousand dollars. It would be sweet revenge!

Kareem was a pretty big New York supplier who dealt in ice, Ecstasy, and ketamine. From what I remembered, he told me he had beat the feds several years back.

Boss looked at me. "Kareem Abbas, I know him. He's from New York, right?" *Wow,* I thought. *How much do they know?* They began to ask about my dealings with Kareem—how I met him, what I bought from him, when I'd see him. Even though it had been a while since I'd contacted Kareem, our dealings were still recent enough to interest the agents.

"Tell you what," said one agent, after about twenty minutes of questioning. "We're gonna give you a little break for being so forthcoming about Kareem and volunteering all the information from the filing cabinet and fax machine. So we're not going to book you tonight. But tomorrow, you're gonna come to our office in the federal building on Spring Street, to the eighth floor, at 10:00 a.m. Got it? Don't be late.

"If you don't show up, we'll have a search warrant out for your arrest, and we'll come after you...and hunt you down." I looked up at him and knew I didn't have any other option.

— — —

I woke up the next morning after a fitful sleep. I was afraid to call anyone, thinking my phone might be tapped. I didn't go out; where was I going to go? I looked around the room and was hoping that what had happened the day before was really a nightmare. I walked to my closet and looked in my safe. Bare as a bone. Not only was I facing another meeting with federal agents, but also I didn't have any drugs for my regular morning pick-me-up. I found one glass pipe and put it to my lips, just to smoke what little residue was left in it. Not even enough to give me a buzz.

I looked at the clock: 9:35 a.m. I needed to be at the DEA's office at

10:00, so I jumped up and started to get ready. I didn't know what to bring, what to wear, what to expect. Were they going to lock me up right then? Would I be able to call someone? Should I call a lawyer? Time was ticking away and getting closer to 10:00. I jumped in my car and sped toward downtown. This was it. I was on my way to meet my fate.

I arrived at the office on the eighth floor. They took me into a small room and began asking more questions. After a few hours, they told me to come back the following week and said they'd be watching me. Then, to my surprise, they let me walk out. I had no idea what this all meant.

They had taken all my money and my inventory of drugs. Without money and with nothing to sell, it meant no more shopping sprees, no more flying across the country with friends, no more throwing huge, extravagant parties. I was supposed to live a normal life—except that I was completely broke.

— — —

The first few weeks after I got busted, I tried to make an honest living by promoting my Sunday tea dances. But the only thing that had made the parties sustainable was the drug dealing. I barely broke even on the cover charge at the door, and often I lost money. I needed money each week to fly in the DJ, to pay the graphic designer and order the fliers. But that's difficult when you don't have any money.

So I tried to sell a small amount of drugs just to survive. I was scared to use my phone, so I would use a pay phone to make calls to my suppliers. But no one would touch me. Word had spread that I'd gotten busted. I spent most of my time making up stories and trying to cover up the fact that the DEA had raided my place. Few believed me; even my loyal customers didn't want anything to do with me.

I was forced to move way down the food chain and buy from sketchy dealers who used to work for me. I could sense the satisfaction in their eyes as they doled out drugs that I was paying for. I felt like a beggar: "More, please." The tables had turned—now the king had become a serf.

I was spiraling down into a place I had never experienced before. The dark haze of depression colored my days and nights, and I tried to shake it by smoking more ice. The drugs I bought to sell ended up in my pipe. I was starting to go without sleep for up to ten days, strung out on ice. Then my body would finally collapse, and I'd sleep for one or two days straight.

— — —

Smoking ice made me desire sex more than food, so I started frequenting bathhouses. A bathhouse exists for only one reason: anonymous sex between gay men. It's typically a back-alley, hole-in-the-wall kind of place. I'd always go alone—no one goes there to socialize. There was one off Fourth Street in Atlanta. The front door was around the back facing the interstate. I'd enter quickly from my car to try to avoid being seen.

Coming into the bathhouse, I'd enter a room the size of a walk-in closet—so small that two people had a hard time squeezing past each other. To the right was a window of thick glass. I'd slide my ID and some money—thirty dollars—under the glass, and someone inside would buzz me in. The dimly lit hallway had tiny rooms on both sides, each with a foam mattress on a plywood platform. The rooms were moldy and dank, smelling of sweat, steam, and more sweat. I'd often lie to myself, saying that I'd just stop in for a moment and leave after one encounter. But eight hours—and countless, nameless faces—later, I was at the desk paying thirty dollars for another eight hours.

One early April morning, after another bathhouse marathon, I sat with a friend in his room. I knew he had some ice, so I asked if I could get a hit. As I pulled out my glass pipe, he pulled out his baggie.

He looked at me kind of aloof when he saw my pipe. "Oh, you smoke tina? What a waste," he said as he handed me the baggie of ice. "You don't know what you're missing."

At first I didn't know what he was talking about, then realized what he meant as he pulled out a syringe. I put some ice into my pipe and began to smoke, then sat uncomfortably watching the ritual before me. I certainly wasn't afraid of needles, but I had never seen anybody shoot up—especially this close.

He set a bent spoon on the plywood base of the bed and dropped several shards of ice into the spoon. After filling his syringe with water from a vial out of his bag, he slowly squirted it into the spoon, and the shards quickly dissolved.

"Now that's some pure stuff," he explained. "See, nothing floating. Beautiful." His eyes fixated on the spoon, and he started licking his lips. "I can already feel the tingle in the back of my throat."

He took a bit of cotton and dropped it into the spoon. Then he placed the needle in the middle of the cotton and drew up the water. Pointing the needle upward, he flicked it a few times to get the bubbles out. He pulled out a rubber tube and tied it around his arm as he clenched and unclenched his fist. As he did this, I saw the track marks on his arm—the scarring from all the injections he had done. It sent a shiver down my spine.

He slapped his arm a few times as he searched for a vein. "Ahhh, here's one," he said, eying a small, thin line on his forearm as he wiped it clean with an alcohol swab. He picked up the syringe and inserted the needle. I saw a little blood enter the syringe as he pulled back on the plunger.

"Now this'll burn a bit, but boy, it's worth it." He exhaled and slowly injected the contents of the syringe into his arm. With the needle still stuck in his arm, he released the rubber tube and whispered, "Five... four...three...two..."

He didn't even make it to one before his body turned white and his eyes rolled back in his head, revealing only the whites. He let out a long, slow sigh, and his body went limp.

He lay there motionless for what seemed to be forever. I began to panic. He wasn't moving and he wasn't breathing. I leaned forward and nervously shook him. Nothing. I shook again, a little harder.

"Hey…hey…hey!" I shook his leg harder and harder. *"Hey!"* Then his eyes rolled forward, he coughed weakly, and he gasped for air.

He looked at me through the thin slits of his closed eyes and smirked. "Now that's how you slam tina." He pulled the needle out of his arm and sighed, "Oh, that was good."

— — —

In June, I received a letter from the United States Attorney's Office. It was a court date for July 17, 1998. *What?* I read the letter through, then again. I thought because I was cooperating with the DEA, everything would be taken care of. I picked up the phone and called the DEA agent I was working with.

"I got this letter in the mail," I said, explaining what was written in it. "So, what's this all about? Do I have to go to court?"

"Yeah. You gotta do whatever it says."

"Do I need a lawyer?"

"I can't tell you about that. I'm not supposed to give you any legal advice. That's on you."

"I thought we had a deal."

"Hey, I gotta go." Before I knew it, the line went dead. I quickly realized what this meant. *It's a dog-eat-dog world. Every man for himself.*

The court date rolled around, and I showed up with a free attorney because I couldn't afford to pay for one. The judge read my charge— "conspiracy to possess methamphetamine with intent to distribute"— then asked me what was my plea. *Are you serious?* I thought. *They caught me red-handed!* So I pled guilty and was ordered to pretrial supervision starting the following week. This meant weekly meetings with a probation officer—and weekly drug tests.

If only I could switch out my dirty urine and use someone else's, I'd be set. But where would I find clean urine? All the people I knew were users. But after some searching around, I found an acquaintance of an acquaintance of an acquaintance who didn't use drugs. He gave me a good supply in a plastic water bottle. I kept it chilled in the refrigerator and marked it *Don't drink!*

On the day of my test, I got a small Elmer's glue bottle, which was washed clean, and filled it with the substitute urine. Since the urinalysis cups have thermometers on them to reveal whether the sample was body temperature, I warmed up the urine in a microwave and then put it in my underwear, where I kept it warm and easily accessible.

When it came time to do the test, a probation officer went into the bathroom with me and stood there to watch. The officer had to see the urine actually leave my body and enter the cup. There was a mirror against the wall next to the toilet so that the officer could see from both sides. It's already uncomfortable to pee with someone staring at you, but it's even harder when you're trying to sneak someone else's urine into the sample cup. Even though the Elmer's glue bottle gave a stream that looked real, there was one problem. Air needed to suck back into the bottle in order to release all the contents.

No problem, I thought. "I'm kind of nervous...pee shy," I told the officer. "Can I turn on the water?"

As water ran in the sink next to the toilet, I very gingerly pulled the glue bottle out through my fly and held it in my hand—away from the eyes of the officer. I delicately twisted the orange cap with my fingers, and as I squeezed I let out a well-timed sigh. I was quite proud of myself—especially when I passed the test.

— — —

One day I woke up with a gnawing hunger. I looked at my clock and saw 6:43. Was it a.m. or p.m.? I got out of bed and pulled back the blinds. The sun was beginning to set. I walked into the bathroom and splashed water on my face. I looked in the mirror and saw my emaciated body. *Well, at least I'm ripped.* I got on the scale: 136 pounds. Sure, I'd lost forty pounds, but I'd be the envy of any Weight Watchers group!

I heard my front door open. "Hey, Chris." It was a familiar voice.

"Jack! So glad you're here. Just in time to crack on," I said as I walked to the kitchen and pulled out my glass pipe.

But before I could pour some ice into the bowl, he said, "Uh, that's okay. I don't want any."

"What? You've got to be kidding me. Are you feeling all right?" I said jokingly.

"No, seriously. I'm trying to cut back." Jack was a student at Georgia Tech and had to deal with real life. "I brought you some dinner." He put a takeout box from Cowtippers on my kitchen counter. "It's your favorite: filet mignon cooked medium—just the way you like it—caesar salad and baked sweet potato."

It had been a long time since I'd had a steak from Cowtippers. In fact, it had been a while since the last time I had eaten. I was famished.

"Besides," Jack continued, "you need to take care of yourself."

"What? Are you trying to mother me?" I said, stuffing my mouth with a piece of steak.

Jack laughed uncomfortably. "Well, um…I'd better get going," he said, as he shifted his weight from one foot to the other.

"But you just got here," I said, swallowing a mouthful of sweet potato. "It's still early, and the night is young."

Jack looked down, obviously uncomfortable. "Yeah, I've got somewhere to go."

"Where?"

"A party."

"Who's having a party?" I asked, setting my fork on the counter.

Jack looked at his hands, avoiding eye contact. "You know…just some guys."

Just some guys. Unbelievable. Now Jack was going to parties that I wasn't invited to? That was a switch. I had been at the top of the A-list in Atlanta. If there was a private party in Atlanta's gay community, I was invited. If there was a line of people waiting outside a club, I didn't have to wait. Jack was my best friend, and I brought him everywhere I went.

But now Jack—Jack, my best friend—was going to parties that nobody had mentioned to me.

I knew that my reputation and new habits were making me an embarrassment to my friends, who were keeping me at arm's length. But I knew I still had Jack, my best friend. Or so I thought.

"I'll call you tomorrow. Okay, honey?"

He walked out the door and gently shut it behind him, leaving me standing in my kitchen with my mouth open, ready to protest.

At least I had one friend left. I looked at my glass pipe. *I guess it's just you and me.*

— — —

As the months passed, it was getting harder and harder to keep up with my bills. I wasn't able to pay my thirteen-hundred-dollars-per-month rent, or my car payment, or my phone bill. Few people were willing to front me drugs anymore, and the little ice I got, I smoked. I kept up appearances the best I could for as long as I could, but there were times when I sat in my upscale apartment in Buckhead with nothing to eat— trying to scrounge up enough change just to go out and get a burger.

But it was August, and Hotlanta weekend was coming up. If I could put on one big, successful Sunday tea dance, maybe I could make it after all. This could be the break I'd been needing. Just one year earlier, the party at the Chili Pepper on the Sunday of Hotlanta weekend was incredible! More than three thousand people were there. If just half that number came this year, I'd be able to pay my bills and maybe afford some good drugs.

Some people fronted me some money, using last year as a reference point, and I reserved a venue overlooking Piedmont Park. I booked a well-known Miami DJ, David Knapp, and had cool fliers designed and printed. *If only I can survive until Hotlanta,* I told myself, *everything will be okay. I just have to hang on.*

But my heart sank when I read the official brochure for the Hotlanta festivities. The last event on the schedule was another Sunday tea dance—not mine. Anybody who bought the hundred-dollar pass for the weekend would automatically have a ticket to that party. Who would come to mine—especially if they had to pay extra?

As a result, "Chris Yuan Presents Ice 1998" was dismal. It was held in a cheesy banquet hall. I couldn't afford a good sound system, so the sound—and the lights—were tragic. David Knapp was fierce, but he was working under impossible conditions. The floor of the DJ booth shook with the vibrations of people dancing. It shook when Motion, our local drag queen, did her number. And every time it shook, the music skipped. It was like a bad birthday party at a roller rink. There were barely a hundred people there. I couldn't wait for the night to be over.

A handful of my remaining friends had come to support me. At the end of the night, we stood around and I pretended nothing was wrong. I could tell they were embarrassed for me, knowing what a tragic party it was and how I had lost lots of money. But I didn't want their pity.

"Hey! Guess what time it is?" I said. "Crack on!"

They all sympathetically crammed into a bathroom stall with me—trying to cheer me up. And as we clicked on our butane torches, someone busted through the door. "Chris! They're towing your car!"

I ran out to the parking lot just in time to see a tow truck pull out of the lot into the street, with my Prelude behind it. I hadn't paid the note on it in months, and the bank must have heard about my party. I turned around, and my friends and a few others stood looking at me and watching my car being towed away. It was like I could hear their thoughts:

"Poor Chris, he can't even pay his bills."

"It's so sad."

"This party was a flop, and now they've taken his car? How pathetic."

I fell to the ground, the rough gravel cutting my knees. My head dropped into my hands, and I started to cry.

Nineteen

Count Your Blessings

Angela: December 9, 1998

It was a brisk, wintery afternoon as I drove home from Bible Study Fellowship. The sun shone brightly in a powder-blue sky, and I was singing along to Moody Radio in my car. "Count your blessings, name them one by one."[14] So I did. I counted my blessings as I drove, and my heart was full of them. My cup was overflowing with the joy of Christmas, with the joy of friendship, with the joy of a marriage that was coming back to life from the ashes. *So many things to be thankful for,* I thought, as I parked the car in our garage and headed into the house.

I hadn't even made it through the door when the telephone rang. I ran over and picked it up.

"Hello?"

Click.

A prerecorded voice said, "This is the Atlanta City Detention Center. You have a collect call from"—there was a brief pause, then a familiar voice—"Chris Yuan."

I hadn't heard Christopher's voice in months—but from jail? Hearing it now caused mixed emotions: joy that he'd called, anxiety that he was in jail, fear of the unknown. I held my breath and clutched the phone.

The recording continued. "If you would like to accept this collect call, please press 1. If you would like to refuse this collect call, please press 2. If you would like to block this caller from calling again, please press..." There was no hesitation. I quickly punched 1.

Click.

The noise and clamor of people in the background rushed through the receiver. "Hey...Mom?" The sound that came through was soft and uncertain. The tone of Christopher's voice was different. The usual anger, resentment, and arrogance were absent. Instead, there was softness and sadness.

"Mom...I'm in jail."

I paused, uncertain of what to say. I had never expected that he would wind up in jail. I'd never even known anybody who'd been in jail. Never before had I seen or driven past a jail. I just imagined thieves and crooks and murderers and rapists in a dark dungeon. It was hard for me not to be scared for my son's life. And yet I knew that somehow God was in control. Besides, I had prayed, *Lord, do whatever it takes.*

"Son, are you okay?" I asked.

I wasn't so much concerned about why he was in jail, but I simply wanted to hear from his heart. For too long Leon and I had been walled off from Christopher's life, his feelings, his innermost thoughts. I wanted to be able to get a glimpse of all that again.

There was silence on the other end of the line.

"Yeah...I'm all right."

After a brief pause, Christopher began to explain what had happened. He told me that his apartment had been raided by federal drug agents in January. Then the court placed him on pretrial release, which included weekly urinalysis tests. But he failed three tests in four weeks, so the judge revoked his bond, and he was taken into custody earlier that morning. My mind was reeling with all the information. Certainly, I'd prayed, *Whatever it takes.* But I had never imagined it might involve drugs or jail.

Christopher talked and I listened for several more minutes. This was the longest conversation we'd had in years, and I treasured every moment. It didn't matter where he was or what led to his arrest. I finally felt an openness and willingness in his spirit. And that was a miracle.

A recording interrupted our conversation: "This call will end in one minute."

"I'm only allowed fifteen minutes," Christopher explained. I couldn't believe how those moments flew by. "There's a line of guys behind me. Mom…I wish we could talk longer, but I gotta go. Can I call back later?"

"Yes, definitely." I couldn't believe that he wanted to talk more. Of course we'd accept his phone call again, no matter what time, no matter what the cost. After all those years of resistance, this was a dream come true. Although the fifteen minutes passed by quickly, they were so precious.

"I'll come down to see you in the next few days," I said. "Call again and I'll let you know my travel arrangements." I paused. "Christopher, I want you to know that Dad and I are going to walk with you through this, okay? I love you."

"Thanks, Mom… Love you too… Bye."

Click.

As I hung up the phone and the tears welled up in my eyes, I knew that I had to look beyond my present circumstances, look beyond today's storm, look beyond the trial I was in and instead, rejoice. I remembered Romans 5:3–5:

> We also rejoice in our sufferings, because we know that suffering
> produces perseverance; perseverance, character; and character,
> hope. And hope does not disappoint us, because God has poured
> out his love into our hearts by the Holy Spirit, whom he has
> given us.

I felt compelled to thank God for what he was doing in Christopher's life, even though I hurt for him like never before. And I knew without a doubt—with complete certainty—that this was God's answer to my

Christopher Yuan

This is my list of blessings that began with Christopher's incarceration on December 9, 1998. As his years in prison passed, I kept expanding the list by using more adding-machine tape. Today it's longer and taller than I am.

prayers. *Count your blessings, name them one by one,* went through my head again. *Yes,* I thought. *That is what I must do.*

I looked in Leon's business office and saw an adding machine. I pulled a small piece of adding machine tape and grabbed a pen. I scribbled down these first blessings so I wouldn't forget that God was still at work.

"Christopher is in a safe place, and he called us for the first time."

A warmth and indescribable peace enveloped me, as I closed my eyes and thanked God. With gratefulness in my heart, these words floated through my mind:

Turn your eyes upon Jesus
Look full in his wonderful face
And the things of earth will grow strangely dim
In the light of his glory and grace.[15]

Twenty

Out of the Trash

Christopher: December 12, 1998

Sleep. The opiate of the hopeless. The bed was hard, and the plastic-covered mattress crackled every time I moved. A rough wool blanket was all I had for warmth on this cold December day. It wasn't long enough to cover my whole body, and it hardly stopped the draft that seemed to blow from every corner of the room.

Lying on a hard metal bunk in jail, I knew that opening my eyes would only remind me of the grim situation I was in. Only in the darkness of my mind could I escape the pain of this new, haunting reality. I lingered behind closed eyelids in the comfort of darkness and pulled the rough blanket to my chin. *If I don't open my eyes and just keep sleeping, maybe I'll wake up to find that this was only a miserable nightmare.*

But my eyes betrayed me. As they cracked open, I couldn't ignore the hard cinder block and cold iron of my six-by-ten-foot cell. A little daylight filtered through the dirty, bulletproof sliver of a window. I assumed I'd slept another ten or twelve hours. The guards had taken my watch from me. In its place I'd been given time…hard time.

I got up to use the metal toilet at the foot of the bed and looked up at the small piece of steel on the wall that served as a mirror. The reflection was cloudy and distorted, but I could still see my dark eyes and sunken cheeks. I flushed the toilet, then pulled up my orange jumpsuit and tied the arms of it, beltlike, around my waist. I pushed open the cell door and walked into the common area.

Just outside my door, I almost tripped over a stack of meal trays that still had food on them. A Hispanic guy was walking by my cell. *"Vato,"* he said. "We thought you were dead in there." I gave him a confused look. He went on, "We kept looking in on you, man, but you weren't moving."

"What time is it?" I asked.

"About two o'clock in the afternoon, amigo," he said. "And it's Saturday." He laughed as he walked to his cell.

Saturday? How could it be Saturday?

It was Wednesday when I had seen my probation officer and she revoked my bond. Sure, I failed three drug tests. I guess I was out of second chances…again. The first two fails were because the guy who supplied me with supposedly "clean" urine had had his wisdom teeth pulled and had taken a painkiller with codeine. For some reason, my sample had to be taken to a lab, so the positive test result for codeine hadn't come back until my next urinalysis. By then, it was too late; I'd already given them another cup of codeine-rich urine. I failed two drug tests for something I didn't even take!

So I'd decided to try another route. There was a drink that was supposed to mask the drugs in urine. I took it and drank gallons of water before the test. But it didn't work. The test came back positive for meth. I guess I had smoked too much ice—there was no hiding it. That was less than a week before I landed in the Atlanta City Detention Center.

I'd wound up here on a Wednesday afternoon, following several days and nights without sleep. Once in jail, I had crashed right after calling my mom and having my first jail dinner. The next day, without any meth, I was dragging and barely made it to lunch. I passed out again right after lunch. I must have slept through dinner on Thursday and all day Friday. That's why there were six meal trays outside my door. I looked at the food on the trays and the bugs flying and crawling about. I was hungry, but not that hungry.

I looked at the forty or so men in our pod, 3 South East Block #5. They gathered in the common area, playing cards, watching television, or just shuffling around in their flip-flops. The men looked rough, like guys living on the street. One with tattoos and a mouthful of gold walked by. *Now, he looks like a real drug dealer,* I thought. Another guy had one pant leg of his orange jumpsuit rolled up with the other one dragging on the ground. *Gangbanger,* I thought. I'd best stay far away from these criminals. Fortunately, my mother was coming to visit me later that night, and I could get out of the pod—at least for a moment.

I was in survival mode as I paced along the perimeter of the cellblock, steering clear of any interaction with the other men. I turned to walk back toward my cell when I passed a garbage can overflowing with trash. I realized that my life was just like that trash. I had grown up in an upper-middle-class suburb of Chicago, my dad had two doctorates, and I'd been on my way to becoming a doctor myself. Now I found myself living among common criminals—trash.

Not even my friends wanted me. They wouldn't even accept a collect call. I was nothing more than a reject, a throwaway. I took a deep breath and let out a sigh as my shoulders slumped and I dropped my head. I was about to turn back toward my cell when something on top of the trash caught my eye.

I bent over and picked up a Gideon's New Testament. It was brand-new and not even opened. I carried it back to my cell and thought, *I've got a ton of time on my hands. I might as well have something to do.* As I sat on the metal bunk's cold mattress, I opened the small book to the gospel of Mark.

Twenty-One

Don't Let Me Cry

Angela: December 12, 1998

I was awake before my alarm rang. As I lay in bed, the thought of actually going to visit a jail sent a chill up my spine. I'd never been to such a place before. Everything I pictured about jails came from my imagination—cold, dark, haunting. But I knew that no matter where I went, God would never leave my side.

I put on my slippers and robe and went into my prayer closet. I opened the Bible to Isaiah 41:10.

> So do not fear, for I am with you;
>> do not be dismayed, for I am your God.
> I will strengthen you and help you;
>> I will uphold you with my righteous right hand.

God had known just what I needed to hear as I faced a difficult and uncertain situation. I was ready to accomplish whatever God had planned for me, knowing that he would uphold me with his righteous right hand.

At six o'clock that evening, Stan Singleton met me outside the Atlanta airport. Stan was a big man but very warm and friendly—kind of like a life-size teddy bear. He was a Christian lawyer—a friend of a friend—who had begun to help Christopher with some basic legal mat-

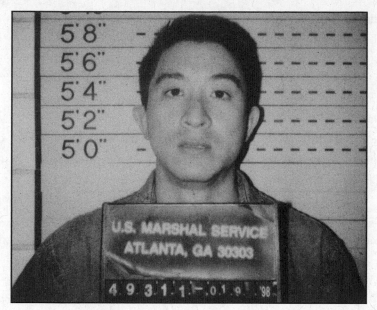

Christopher's booking picture was taken on December 9, 1998, a few days before I visited him at the Atlanta City Detention Center.

ters, pro bono. Stan was a corporate lawyer specializing in nonprofits, but more than that, he was a southern gentleman with a quiet demeanor and a gentle voice. Even though I'd never met him before that evening, his very presence put me at ease and calmed my nerves. The fears I'd felt rising up before leaving home slipped away from me. What a blessing! I made a mental note to add it to my list of blessings.

We walked out into the crisp, winter night as a starry sky greeted us. Stan drove me straight from the airport to the Atlanta City Detention Center. It was a large gray building, ten stories high, occupying an entire city block like a fortress of concrete. Unlike other buildings nearby, it had no windows along the sides—only thin slits peeping through cold cement. Stan pulled his car into a parking lot next to the rail station.

There were no people out walking. The sidewalk and parking lot were empty. It was early evening, but the vacant streets and dark shadows made me press in under Stan's safe shadow. I thanked God that he was there—like my guardian angel.

We passed by a small yellow building—the size of a trailer house—with a red neon sign hanging from its window: *A&B Bonding*. As we crossed the street and approached the entrance to the detention center, I saw a couple of unmarked police cars parked directly below a *No Parking* sign. Security cameras were positioned everywhere—at the crosswalk, on the streetlamps, along the sidewalks, at each corner of the building, and at the entrance.

Inside, it was obvious that no money had been spent on decorations or furnishings. The place was bare concrete—the walls, the floors, the ceiling were all concrete. The flickering fluorescent bulbs spread a pale bluish hue across the empty room. The air was still and smelled stale, like a dank basement.

We walked to the plate glass that protected a small reception enclosure, and Stan spoke politely to a lady who didn't even bother looking up at us. "I'm an attorney for inmate Chris Yuan. I'm here with my client's mother, who flew in from out of town. I have arranged for her to visit with her son."

"What's the inmate's name?" the woman asked without raising her head.

"Chris Yuan," Stan said.

"Can you spell that?"

"Y-u-a-n."

After looking through some papers, she pulled one out and asked for identification. I gave my driver's license to Stan, and he slid both our IDs under the glass. The lady looked them over, eyed the two of us, and slid the IDs back. She then waved her hand toward the end of the room and turned her chair away. Apparently she was done with us.

We heard a loud *clang* from the end of the room, and we stood there, uncertain what to do. The lady behind the glass looked at us, waved, and pointed for me to go through the door. I looked at Stan, and he motioned in the same direction.

"You'll be okay. I'll be here waiting for you."

I walked to the end of the room and through the big metal door. I took a deep breath and stepped forward. *Clang!* The door behind me closed, and I jumped. I was now shut off from the outside and was standing at the end of a long, dark corridor. The polished concrete floor stretched fifty feet in front of me. As the fluorescent lights flickered above, shadows seemed to dance and dart about me. I took a tentative step forward, then another. Slowly I walked along the dark corridor. In any other situation, I would have cried, but tonight I had to be brave for Christopher.

Clong, clong, clong, clong, bang! I jumped again. In front of me a metal gate shook and then slid open automatically. As I walked through the gate, I felt my knees getting weak. I could hardly move forward. Then the *clank* and *rattle* of metal on metal started again as the iron door closed slowly behind me.

"Lord, please carry me," I whispered under my breath. "God, give me strength. Help me to be strong."

I kept walking toward the *clank* and *rattle* in front of me as the next gate opened. There was no one around, not a guard in sight. Only one direction to go, and I hoped that I was being led to the right place. As I passed the second gate, it began to close behind me. This unnerving process repeated itself as I passed through three or four additional sets of iron-bar gates. Security cameras recorded my every step, and I felt myself beginning to tremble. I began to recite the verse that I had read earlier that morning:

> So do not fear, for I am with you;
>> do not be dismayed, for I am your God.
> I will strengthen you and help you;
>> I will uphold you with my righteous right hand.

As I walked down a cold concrete corridor, I knew the only thing carrying me forward was the hand of God. When I finally made it to the end of the hall, a guard opened a door and motioned for me. He took me down a narrow hallway and stopped in front of a small door.

"Wait in here. They'll bring him in shortly."

I paused before I went in. I knew what I was going to see: my precious son, now a prisoner. Was I ready to face this? *Lord, don't let me cry... don't let me cry...please.*

Opening the door, I took a deep breath and then walked in. It was a small room. On the left was a short metal counter that ran along the length of the wall. The wall was divided by partitions into three visiting areas. Above the counter was thick plate glass with wire mesh within. At each station, a metal stool was bolted to the floor, and a phone was available for communicating between inmates and visitors.

I sat on the first stool and looked through the thick glass. On the other side was a similar configuration with stool, divider, and phone— but only enough room for one person to squeeze through.

Ten minutes went by, and finally the door on the other side of the glass opened—and there stood my son.

Christopher was wearing a bright orange jumpsuit. He had a big smile on his face, and I smiled back and waved. The guard unlocked his handcuffs and closed the door. Christopher rubbed his wrists as he shuffled toward the stool. I looked down and saw shackles around his ankles. As he sat down, I looked into his thin face with deep hollows under his cheekbones. I could feel the tears coming. But when I looked into his eyes, I could see the little boy who used to jump in my lap and play at my feet and hug me like he'd never let go. I couldn't help but smile big, as any mother would when seeing her son after such a long time.

We picked up the telephones. I was hoping I could break the ice.

"Christopher!" I said jokingly, "I like your new apartment." He looked at me and laughed.

"Hey, Mom. It's good to see you."

"It's really good to see you too." I asked how he was feeling and about his safety. He told me that he tried to keep to himself to avoid trouble. He told me about how hungry he was. The food wasn't so good and the portions were small. My heart hurt that I couldn't give him anything to eat. He asked if Dad and I would put money in his inmate account so he could buy snacks from the commissary. I was amazed to see how eager he was to talk with me.

"Can you call my friends Jack and Billy?" Christopher asked. "I need to find a place to store my stuff..."

He was talking as if all this was no big deal, as if he would be getting out soon. I think he was hoping for probation or maybe that the judge would send him to the federal prison camp in Atlanta. I had no idea what Christopher was charged with or how bad it was, but I nodded my head, happy to sit there and listen to my son talk.

"I brought some family pictures," I said. "Would you like to see them?" Christopher nodded. I held them up to the glass one by one. I wanted Christopher to know that he was still an important part of our family. I wanted to remind him that he was loved. I wanted him to see some happy memories from his childhood. Christopher pressed his fingers to the glass, trying to touch each photo.

After fifteen minutes, the guard stuck his head in and told me it was time to wrap things up. I turned back to Christopher. He spoke before I did. "Is it okay if I call you collect?"

"Of course it's okay," I said.

Before the guard could kick me out, I gathered enough courage to ask Christopher something he had vehemently rejected so many times before. "May I pray with you?" I'd brought one of the written prayers I'd prayed every morning for five years. I wanted to pray it aloud to Christopher, so he could hear it with his own ears.

Christopher paused and then nodded. "Okay," he said.

I raised my right hand and touched the glass. Christopher slowly brought his hand to mine. Even though I couldn't feel his hand and we were separated by a thick piece of cold glass, his intimate gesture melted my heart and my eyes welled up with tears.

> Dear Lord, you are Christopher's constant Companion. There is no need that you cannot fulfill. Whether your course for Christopher points to the mountaintop of glorious delight or the valleys of human suffering, you are by Christopher's side. You are ever present with Christopher. You are close beside Christopher. When Christopher treads the dark streets of danger and even when Christopher flirts with death itself, you are there to lean upon. When the pain is severe, you are near to comfort. When the burden is heavy, you are there to lean upon. When depression darkens Christopher's soul, you touch him with eternal hope and joy. And when Christopher feels empty and alone and isolated, you fill the aching vacuum with your power. Christopher's security, O Lord, is in your promise to be near to him always and in the knowledge that you will never let him go. Amen.

I could not hold my tears any longer. Even though my son sat in jail, my heart overflowed with joy and thanksgiving. I was actually praying with my son! That was a miracle.

Today is the beginning of a new day, I thought. *Christopher is in the good, strong hands of our great and mighty Father!*

Twenty-Two

Rock Bottom

Christopher: December 21, 1998

Come on, give me two more!" yelled Chris Cloud, my new workout partner. Sweat dripped off my face as I finished a set of curls.

Chris was a friend I made on the cellblock. Because he had been a football player in high school, he enjoyed working out. We got along right off the bat, and it turned out we had much more in common than just exercise.

Like me, he was busted for dealing ice. Like me, his parents were Christians. Like me, his parents had prayed for him to turn to God. We shared the same first name, and, unbelievably, the same birthday in the same year. Chris kept joking that this was more than coincidence and maybe God was up to something. He was raised in the church, but said that only recently had he started taking his faith seriously. We began studying the Bible together—along with our daily workouts.

Without weights in our cellblock, it took some creativity to find substitutes. We got empty trash bags, doubled them up, filled them with water, and tied them to the ends of a broomstick. They served duty as an odd-looking barbell. Each gallon of water weighed about eight pounds, and each bag could hold three to four gallons. Not much weight, but it was better than nothing. The real problem was trying to balance the swishing water while doing reps. We did curls, shoulder presses, and squats. We also incorporated pull-ups off a door frame—using wet rolls of newspaper as grips—and lots and lots of push-ups. We called our makeshift gym the C&C Muscle Factory.

Chris was finishing his set of curls when I heard the *clank* and *rattle* of the cellblock gate. Footsteps followed, then the rattling of keys and familiar drawl of one of the guards.

"You-awn! You-awn! Nurse call!"

Chris set down the water bags. "I think the CO is calling you." These letters stood for "corrections officer."

I walked into the common area, where the guard looked at me and said, "Hey, You-awn! Let's go! Nurse call!"

Nurse call? I thought. *I just went last week.* I went to my cell and grabbed my shoes from under the bunk, having learned early that you never question an officer. As I was pulling up my bright orange jumpsuit, Chris walked in.

"That's strange nobody else is going with you. They always send a group of inmates together over to the hospital for nurse call. I wonder what's up?"

"Yeah, I know. It's kinda strange. We'll finish our workout when I get back, okay?"

The guard banged on my door. "You-awn! Let's move it. Now!"

I scrambled out of my cell and passed the usual scene: inmates clustered around a few card-slamming games of spades and the rest sitting in front of the television, watching soaps or, better yet, *Oprah.*

I stood in front of the gate as the guard handcuffed me, locked the cuffs to a chain around my waist, and shackled my feet. I still wondered why no other inmates were going for nurse call, but it didn't bother me much. At least I was getting outside and out of the cellblock for a while.

My stomach and neck tightened against the cold wind that whipped around my jumpsuit as I climbed into the back of an armored van. The guard signaled a gloved hand to the driver that all was clear for him to head out.

I sat alone in the back of the van and looked through the metal mesh that covered the window. Outside was a beautiful sight: freedom. There was nothing unusual on the Atlanta streets that morning as we waited in downtown traffic. People sat indifferently in their cars, headed to their destinations—oblivious of the privilege they enjoyed just being out and about in the world. The van pulled up to the back of the hospital. I could see streetlamps decorated with boughs of evergreens and candy canes. I waited for the guard to unlock the door. He put down a stool for me to step onto—awkwardly—with my shackled feet.

Despite the frigid wind that took away my breath, I paused in the open air. For a moment, I felt free. I closed my eyes and took in a long, deep breath. Fresh air had never smelled so sweet.

"You-awn, let's go!"

A quick pull on my arm and the rattling of chains forced me back to reality as I was shoved through the clinic's back door. The all-too-familiar glow of artificial light infected the clinic as it did the prison. I looked behind me as the sun's rays of hope disappeared with the closing of the door.

I was pushed into a chair and told to wait. The guard pulled out his keys and uncuffed my right hand. I straightened up, waiting for my other hand to be released. But he quickly took the empty cuff and cranked it around the arm of the chair before walking away.

"Hey, ladies." He smiled at the nurses behind a desk adorned with silver tinsel, and their conversation was reduced to murmurs and bursts of laughter.

A half hour passed. I could see a clock on the far wall. Nurses walked past without even a glance. I was an inmate, a reject of society. I was now less than human. It was as if I didn't exist.

Another ten minutes passed.

Hurry up and wait. In the end, that was what life in jail was reduced to. Everywhere I was taken, I had to wait. But what were a few more minutes? All I had now was time.

A nurse walked toward me, holding a chart in her hand. Her head was down, and her feet dragged on the linoleum floor. She stopped in front of me and looked at my chart.

"Are you 49311-019...Chris Yuan?" she asked.

Reduced to a number. I nodded.

She motioned for the guard to uncuff me from the chair, permitting me to be free of handcuffs as she escorted me into her office.

With my feet still shackled, I dropped into the chair she pointed to as she shut the door. It was obvious that something was not right. I could see strain and discomfort on her face, and I wondered why she was so uneasy.

"You came in last week for your physical," she began, struggling with her words. She opened my chart and flipped past a few pages, then slowly closed it.

"And...well, I..." She cleared her throat and looked down; she had difficulty even making eye contact. "I'm not the one who usually does this."

Does what?

"This physical last week, all the intake inmates had tests done and the blood tests..." She stopped midsentence. She looked at the chart again. "The results..."

She touched a trembling hand to her forehead and moved it through her hair. Looking down again at the desk, she despondently picked up a pen and slowly wrote something on a piece of paper. Laying the pen aside, she slid the paper across the desk toward me.

I looked down and saw three letters and a symbol. What I saw would change my life forever.

HIV+

There was a time I assumed I'd been infected, but I'd never truly dealt with what that meant for me. I hadn't even gone to the trouble of getting tested. I had always managed to keep the idea of it tucked away in the back of my mind, which was numbed by the effects of illicit drugs. But now, just as I felt like I was coming alive again, just as I felt like there was a glimmer of hope, just as I felt like I was reconnecting with my family—I faced this death sentence.

Twenty-Three

It Is Well

Angela: December 21, 1998

Christmas was just four days away. The dental office was decorated with a Christmas tree and a beautiful Nativity scene. Carols filtered through the PA system in the lobby, where a few patients sat waiting to see Leon. I was humming along as I filed papers in the sleek wooden filing drawers behind the front desk when the phone rang.

"Good afternoon, Dr. Yuan's office. May I help you?"

Click. "This is a collect call from the Atlanta City Detention Center..."

A smile spread across my face, and I quickly accepted the call as I walked to the back of the office. Christopher had been calling almost every day. Being reconnected with our son after so many years—regardless of his predicament—was almost too good to be true.

Click. The racket of prison life barreled through the receiver. "Hey, Christopher. Merry early Christmas!" I said while settling into a chair.

But there was no immediate response. Simply a hesitation.

"Christopher? Hello?" In that half second my heart began to race, and I put a hand to my chest as I held my breath. Something was not right.

"Mom?" he started. His voice was troubled. I could barely hear him speak through the shouting behind him. I pressed my ear to the phone and listened as he began to describe his journey to the hospital earlier that morning, waiting in the clinic, not knowing why he was there, and finally receiving the unexpected, harrowing news.

"Mom, I'm…I'm HIV positive…" His sullen and weak voice trailed off as my body went limp. I felt dizzy, and I couldn't catch my breath. The world seemed to stop as my heart pounded in my chest.

Ever since I received the news in 1993 that my son was gay, I had lived with the constant fear that Christopher might one day catch this deadly virus. I knew very little of his personal life, and he never shared with us who he had been with. But this persistent, dark cloud seemed to loom always in the background.

This worst nightmare was now a reality.

I don't remember much more of the conversation, but when I hung up the phone, I felt like a knife was cutting at my broken heart. Aimlessly, I stumbled up the steps to my bedroom. My legs lost their strength, and with one arm against the wall, I dragged my body into my prayer closet. Under the cross, I fell to my knees as tears blurred my eyes. This affliction was more than any mother could bear. I let out a cry of anguish as my head dropped into my hands. I wept aloud, chest heaving as I gasped for air.

Moments passed, and in the silence of my grief, a melody began to play in my head. The soft and sweet strains of a hymn:

> *When peace, like a river, attendeth my way,*
> *When sorrows like sea billows roll;*
> *Whatever my lot, Thou has taught me to say,*
> *It is well, it is well with my soul.*[16]

I took the hand towel off the hook and wiped away my tears. I thought of Psalm 56:8, which says, "You have taken account of my wanderings; put my tears in Your bottle."[17] God understood my pain and he felt my sorrow. I was not alone.

It is well, it is well with my soul.

Twenty-Four

Hope and a Future

Christopher: January 28, 1999

Register number?"

"49311-019," I said to the R&D officer as I stood in front of him stark naked. I was undergoing my second strip search of the morning—once before leaving the Atlanta City Detention Center and now at the notorious United States Penitentiary in Atlanta. Two hours had passed since we arrived at the R&D Department—receiving and discharge—and we were still getting processed. Hurry up and wait. Nothing new.

It didn't help that I wasn't feeling well—but no one cared about that. The corrections officers were wearing uniforms and warm sweaters. I wasn't sure if I had a cold or the flu, but regardless I was running a fever and my head ached. I couldn't wait to finally lie down. But who knew when that would be?

"Run your fingers through your hair," said the guard. "Open your mouth and move your tongue to the left…to the right." After looking in my mouth, the CO looked into my nose as part of the full-cavity search. I closed my eyes, knowing full well to avoid eye contact with the guards.

All I wanted was to get some clothes on. Standing here exposed in the middle of January would be unpleasant for anybody, even a completely healthy person. But today my fever chills made things that much more unbearable.

"Now, turn your head, and let's look behind and in your ears… Raise your arms in front of you with your palms up, now palms down… Lift your arms all the way up," the guard said as he looked at my armpits. Finally, and this was the most embarrassing part, "Now hold up your family jewels… Turn around and lift up your feet… Okay, now bend over and spread your cheeks." I knew of nothing more degrading than this. But in the past seven weeks of incarceration, and after enduring countless strip searches, I had learned to swallow my pride. What other choice did I have?

USP Atlanta was a high-security prison for men and also a temporary holdover facility for inmates like me who were on their way to the prison where they would begin doing their time. What made USP Atlanta notorious was that it was a twenty-three-hour lockdown facility. That meant being confined to our cells for twenty-three hours a day and being let out for only one hour a day to take a shower, attempt to make a phone call, get clean clothing, or exercise in a caged-in basketball court. At the Atlanta City Detention Center, we had not been allowed out of the cellblock, but we had been allowed to leave our cells during the day to watch television, play cards, eat with other inmates, work out, or just stretch our legs.

"What size?" asked a guard, as I walked down the row to get my prison-issued clothing. Every time an inmate went to a new facility, he got a new set of clothes. We were not allowed to bring anything with us—no clothes, papers, or books.

"Large," I said. I had learned that an inmate's top priority was not the right fit or whether clothes looked good. The top priority was comfort. I grabbed a pair of boxers and socks and slipped them on before grabbing a T-shirt and khaki scrub pants. With clothes on, I finally felt human again—and no more bright orange jumpsuits.

I asked a guard for a paper towel so I could blow my nose. I rubbed my temples, trying to ease the headache. Getting through the flu season in prison was always a challenge. If one inmate got sick, usually the entire cellblock got it. And for someone with a fragile immune system, the flu could be a serious health threat. According to a prison doctor, it could even be a matter of life and death for someone who is HIV positive. The last thing I needed was to catch pneumonia.

After we grabbed pillowcases, sheets, wool blankets, towels, toothbrushes, and soap, we were brought to our cellblock. It was larger than the cellblocks at the Atlanta City Detention Center. This one consisted of a long, wide hall without any common area—just cells. The guard barked for us to follow him. He walked up to a cell, unlocked it, then called off a name from his list. After locking the cell, he moved on to the next.

"Yuan!"

"Here," I responded with a cough and cleared my throat, which had begun to hurt. I shuffled over in my government-issued canvas sneakers.

"Register number."

"49311-019," I replied.

I walked into the cell and placed my sheets and towel on the metal bunk as the door slammed shut behind me. I was glad there was nobody else in the cell. I collapsed onto the bed. *Same hard, plastic-covered mattresses,* I thought. *But at least I can lie down.* I was in no shape to make the bed, so I simply lay there with my head throbbing.

— — —

At my sentencing hearing earlier that month, I had thought I was going to get by with a short sentence—especially because of my HIV status. But the prosecutor, Assistant U.S. Attorney Chelsea O'Brien, had made sure that the judge hadn't forgotten what I was charged with: the equivalent of 9.1 tons of marijuana. With so many different types of illicit drugs in circulation, marijuana was used as the common denominator in federal sentencing guidelines. And 9.1 tons was the amount confiscated from my apartment plus the evidence of my distributing. I was facing a minimum of ten years on up to a maximum of life in prison.

I was sitting on the stand during my sentencing hearing as those numbers were read off. *Ten years to life?* I had looked out over the court-room—empty except for my friend Jack and my parents. *So this is how it all ends,* I thought. Where was my huge group of friends? Where were all the people I thought I could depend on?

I felt dizzy as I stood to receive my sentence. "It is the judgment of the court that the defendant, Christopher Yuan, is hereby committed to the custody of the Bureau of Prisons to be imprisoned for a term of seventy-two months. It's further ordered that..."

Seventy-two months, I thought. *That's six years. Six whole years of my life. Will I even survive the sentence?*

— — —

So there I was, locked in a tiny cell in Atlanta's high-security prison. I looked at the metal bunk above me, laden with graffiti, gang symbols, and obscenities. What did I have to look forward to? Six years of the prime of my life taken away from me. No one would ever plan for his life to come to this—a reject of society, no future to look forward to. Is this what the rest of my life would be like? Sitting in cells as property of the federal government—simply a number?

I scanned the drawings and words on the rusty metal sheet above me, and my eyes were drawn to the far corner. The words were barely legible, and the letters were hastily scribbled. It was messy, but I could make out the words: *If you're bored, read Jeremiah 29:11.*

I looked around the room. There was nothing but a small desk and a chair bolted to the wall. No Bible. On the other side of the room was a metal toilet and sink unit. No Bible. Next to it was a small, rusty locker with a foam cup and a deck of cards on top. I mustered enough energy to sit up and walk to the locker. After opening it up, I dug around and found a few empty cereal boxes, a pad of paper, a couple of foam bowls, and a bunch of napkins. Then my hand hit something in the back. It felt like the corner of a book. I tugged it out—it was a Bible.

I quickly flipped to Jeremiah 29:11 and read, "'For I know the plans

I have for you,' declares the LORD, 'plans to prosper you and not to harm you, plans to give you hope and a future.'"

Hope. A future. Things I didn't have now. Coming out of the nurse's office and my sentencing hearing, I was out of hope. I had no future. I had tried to make myself a future in Louisville and in Atlanta. I had sought out my own plans, my own ways—and all that accomplished was my arrest, incarceration, and a six-year sentence. I would love to prosper, love to have a future.

I kept reading:

"Then you will call upon me and come and pray to me, and
I will listen to you. You will seek me and find me when you
seek me with all your heart. I will be found by you," declares
the LORD, "and will bring you back from captivity. I will gather
you from all the nations and places where I have banished you,"
declares the LORD, "and will bring you back to the place from
which I carried you into exile." (Jeremiah 29:12–14)

The thought that God could restore me and bring me back from captivity resonated deep within my spirit. At this point, the world would be happy for me to be locked away for good. And yet, God was saying something completely different. He wanted to be a part of my life—no matter who I was or what I had done. He didn't see me as a criminal. He didn't see me as a felon. He didn't see me as a number. But rather, he saw me—and he saw hope.

For the rest of my life, I was going to live with this felony on my record—like a permanent stain branded on my soul. But with God it seemed I had no record; I had no debt to be paid; I had no shameful past. I wanted that. Just the possibility of hope and a future seemed to brighten my gloomy cell and improve my dreary morning. Maybe I actually did have something to look forward to.

— — —

It was the afternoon of March 1, 1999. The plane landed at what I assumed—and hoped—to be the airport in Lexington, Kentucky. For security purposes, the guards and marshals never told us where we were going. But I had an idea that my final destination was the Federal Medical Center in Lexington.

I'd spent three-and-a-half grueling weeks at USP Atlanta—more than anyone should ever have to endure. So I was very happy when I was taken out of Atlanta and initially flown to the Federal Transfer Center (FTC) in Oklahoma City on the Justice Prisoner and Alien Transportation System plane—better known as Con Air. The FTC in Oklahoma City was a holdover facility at the western edge of Will Rogers World Airport. It was used for inmates being transported across the country. It wasn't great, but it wasn't a twenty-three-hour lockdown facility like USP Atlanta. Regardless, I was still happy a week later to get out of there to be taken to the "big house" where I'd be able to begin my time.

I guessed that it had to be late in the afternoon, and I was beyond exhausted. We'd been up since early morning. The guards at FTC Oklahoma City banged on our doors around four o'clock in the morning and told us we had fifteen minutes to get ready. After almost four hours of paperwork and being shuffled from holding cell to holding cell, about one hundred of us were stripped down, given another set of clothes, and then bound in chains. All this was done in an assembly-line process.

We stood in a single-file line. First, a chain was put around our waists. Then we were handcuffed, and the cuffs were looped through the chain. Finally, we stood on a wooden platform so the guards could easily put shackles around our ankles. The sound of a hundred inmates moving along a hallway, single file with chains dragging, was certain to rouse anyone who still felt groggy.

— — —

We had flown to three other airports, but I couldn't figure out what airports or even the states we had been in. We had waited in the plane as it sat on the Tarmac for about an hour each time we landed. A bus would drive out to drop off and pick up inmates. There were about a dozen United States marshals on this plane, and several went out with shotguns in their hands. I looked outside as they circled the airplane and prepared each exchange of inmates.

At lunch time, the marshals handed out sack lunches. I was hungry, but I'd learned to be careful what I ate while traveling. The last thing I needed was digestive issues while in chains on Con Air—especially since the bathroom door remained open while a marshal kept an eye on you.

We tried to eat our lunches, but because of the handcuffs, we had to lean forward, our chests in our laps, bringing our mouths down to the ham or egg-salad sandwiches. It was clumsy, and a few of the guys spilled their drinks in their laps. I decided to leave the juice alone—better to be thirsty than ride all day with soggy—and later, sticky—pants.

About a half hour after we landed, a bus finally pulled up. I looked out the window and watched guards bring out the inmates who would board our plane. A marshal stood and began calling out names of prisoners who were being taken off the plane. When he was finished, about twenty of us exited through the back door. I moved carefully and managed not to trip on my ankle shackles or plant my face onto the concrete Tarmac below while deplaning.

The Boeing 727 was white, unmarked, and discreet—but suspicious enough. The plane loomed above us with its engines blaring. The marshals confirmed our identification and patted us down one last time—just for good measure. We boarded a bus, and I began looking for clues as to where I was.

As soon as I heard the guards speak, there was no mistaking their Kentucky drawl. And as we hit the highway, signs reading *Lexington* and the Kentucky license plates around us confirmed that I was back in the Bluegrass State. Not a single inmate missed the scenery flying by us. I pressed my head against the black metal mesh that covered the windows and gazed outside. I tried to take in as much as I could of the roads, houses, highways, and fields before it was all taken away from me again.

Twenty minutes later, as the sun shone low in the winter sky, our bus pulled into the drive leading to the Federal Medical Center in Lexington. Like most prisons, it was out in the country. Our bus had traveled through miles of open fields and rolling hills. I had forgotten how beautiful the countryside looked, even in the dead of winter.

When we arrived, the clock read 4:35 p.m. Our intake processing took the entire evening, and we were given dinner in foam boxes. We had to go through all the usual R&D procedures, but since this was our final destination, there was more paperwork and more prison-issued clothing and more information to be recorded. Four hours later, we were finally released from R&D and taken to our units.

The buildings were old—like something out of the 1920s. FMC Lexington used to be called the U.S. Narcotics Farm for drug addicts. The compound was huge, covering more than one thousand acres of land. It certainly beat a six-by-ten-foot cell or a locked-down cellblock. The buildings were massive red-brick and moss-darkened concrete structures. A few trees grew in a courtyard boxed in by more buildings.

Six of us were assigned to Bluegrass Unit. Bluegrass was three stories high and shaped like a square U—two long halls connected by a shorter hall. There were no cells, just rooms, and the doors on the rooms didn't have locks. They were a lot like old dorm rooms.

A guard led the six of us to what looked like a storage closet. Inside were three bunk beds and six tall metal lockers. There was no door, so we draped a sheet across the opening. The hall was empty; most of the inmates were in the recreation yard. It was late, but the yard stayed open until 9:45 p.m., when it closed in preparation for the prisonwide count at 10:00 p.m.

The five official counts each weekday—six on weekends—were the institution's way of ensuring accountability of all inmates. Every inmate had to be at his assigned bunk in his assigned unit for all counts. The hallway doors were locked during the count, and we had to stay in our rooms until it was over.

I glanced at the clock: 8:46 p.m. I could still make it out to the yard for an hour, but I had to wait until 8:50 p.m. when the controlled movement started.

Controlled movement was the time allotted for inmates to move from one area of the prison compound to another—whether it was the yard, the commissary, the library, the hobby crafts shop, the medical clinic, even the chapel. It started at ten till the hour and ended at the top of the hour. It was explained to us in R&D that when controlled movement was over, all doors locked shut, and anyone locked out was in for a "shot"—a write-up—or worse, a few days alone in "the hole," the Special Housing Unit. I waited for the guard to open the door, then I followed the other inmates who seemed to be headed to the yard.

Just being able to walk through a set of doors—without handcuffs, without chains, without a guard escort—was so freeing. It turned out that the yard wasn't too far away. I walked through a small, dark hallway, which opened to the recreation yard, and what I saw just about took my breath away.

Compared to the enclosed basketball courts of USP Atlanta, the rec yard here was a wide expanse of freedom. I felt like a little kid just entering Disney World. The March night air was crisp and cold, but I didn't care. All I'd breathed for the past three months was stale, recycled air. This was incredible! The sky above was clear, and a full moon hung low on the horizon. There seemed to be thousands upon thousands of stars in the heavens. I could have spent the entire night lying on the ground counting stars. It was almost too much to take. I felt like crying.

"Hey, come on, let's walk around the track," said one of the guys who had flown in with me. He pulled on my arm and jerked me back to reality.

We walked the track, first around the empty softball field, then past a fenced-in soccer field. Off in the distance, just a couple hundred feet away, was the women's prison camp. The two facilities were separated by a double fence of barbed wire encircling the yard and the rest of the men's prison compound. We walked past a tennis court and a few handball courts, then finally two basketball courts. People were having fun and acting as if they were carrying on with life. This was just unbelievable. But even more incredible was the fact that I could see no guards, only the one by the door.

As we completed the one-third-mile lap around the track, I told the guys I was going to the weight pile in the middle of the yard. Surrounded by a ten-foot-high fence, the weight pile was nothing fancy. Barbells, plates, benches, racks, and some dumbbells were strewn about the cracked rubber mats covering the ground. The equipment had to have been decades old. The iron was rusted, cracked, and chipped. The bars were bent and the benches wobbly. Few of the benches still had cushions, leaving bare, splintering wood exposed. It looked as if the equipment had broken and the inmates tried to fix it—probably because the prison wasn't going to replace it. Several of the dumbbells had the weights welded on because the holding screws had broken off.

This was no private gym, but it sure beat milk crates full of books and broomsticks with trash bags full of water tied to the ends. I found an empty bench and lay down to look at the sky—still astonished at the beauty above me. As I breathed, the fog coming from my mouth slowly dissipated into the night sky. I placed my hands on the cold barbell and slowly lifted it off the rack. It had been a long time since I had pressed real weight. I lowered the bar, then pumped out reps until I was tired. I lay there speechless, gazing at the sky and listening to the sounds of the yard, the beautiful sounds of people.

Maybe, I thought, *maybe there is the possibility of hope here. Maybe there is a future for me.*

I stayed there for another moment—and smiled. *Yes, just maybe.* I put my hands back on the bar; took in a deep breath of cold, fresh, Kentucky air; and began another set.

Twenty-Five

Beacon of Hope

Angela: March 14, 1999

It was a beautiful, spring Sunday morning in Kentucky as Leon and I left the motel and headed to the prison for our visit with Christopher. He had been in Lexington for two weeks now and had put our names on his visitation list. Driving through rolling hills and blue-green fields, our hearts were full of emotion. This would be our first visit with Christopher face to face, without any glass barrier or courtroom officer.

The drive took us outside Lexington's city limits into the scenic countryside. The air was fresh, and wisps of fog lingered in dew-laden fields. We knew there would be paperwork to fill out, metal detectors to walk through, and other procedures that would take time, so we wanted to get there early. Visiting hours started at 8:30 that Sunday morning, and we pulled into the prison grounds at 7:45.

We were surprised that there was no guard checkpoint as we pulled past the short brick wall, which had a sign indicating it was the Federal Medical Center in Lexington. Leon drove the car another half mile down a road to an empty parking lot for visitors. A huge, red-brick building stood like a fortress spanning the length of three parking lots and rising four stories. The entire compound was surrounded by two sets of twelve-foot-high fences with barbed wire on top and in between.

We parked the car and walked to the entrance door, which was not yet opened. There was a sign with the hours of visitation and a small counter with forms to fill out. We began filling out the forms, and before long other people arrived and lined up behind us. At 8:30 sharp, a guard opened the door. He allowed the first ten people to come in and begin being processed. At this point, a couple dozen people were waiting outside the door. Fortunately, we were first in line.

Leon and I handed the guard behind the desk the filled-out forms and our ID cards. We signed the book with Christopher's name and register number: 49311-019. After our names were confirmed on the visitor list, we went to a small room where we put all our personal items, including my purse, car keys, and cell phone, in a locker. All we could carry in was a clear plastic bag containing a roll of quarters and the key to the storage locker that held our personal belongings. Finally, we stood against the wall in front of a large metal door of the sally port entrance, waiting for enough people to finish being processed so a group of us could walk through the sally port together.

Leon and I looked behind us as a woman in a miniskirt and sleeveless shirt got to the desk. She smiled as she handed the guard her ID and filled-out forms.

The guard looked her up and down and said, "I'm so sorry, ma'am, but no entry. Your skirt must fall below the knee."

"Are you serious?" she said, as her smile vanished. "You don't understand. I ain't got anything else to wear."

"There's a thrift shop just down the road, about five miles."

The woman's bottom lip began to tremble. "You don't understand, sir. I don't have a car, and I only got enough money to catch a cab back to the Greyhound station. You've got to make an exception. Please."

The guard looked past her at the line forming. "I'm gonna need you to move on, ma'am."

"But I come all the way from Mississippi," she said. "I saved my money. I used up my vacation days, and I won't have another chance to see my husband this year."

"I'm really sorry, ma'am. But I don't make the rules," the guard said.

They went back and forth, and another guard came to assist. I really hoped they would just let her in. My heart went out to this lady as she began to cry.

But before we could see the final outcome, a guard motioned to our group standing against the wall. We filed into the middle chamber of the sally port, and a guard behind a thick glass window pressed a button to close the first door. With the first door shut, the second door into the visiting room opened. We filed inside, entering a large room with tables and chairs.

I spotted a small table in the corner near a window, and Leon and I walked straight to it. We sat and waited, focusing our attention on a single white door on the opposite side of the room. The eyes of other visitors were filled with expectation, and the air was almost electric with anticipation. I strained my neck, anxious to catch a glimpse of our son.

Leon and I stood up as the door began to open. A cute little girl with braided and beaded hair yelled, "Mama! Daddy's coming! Daddy's coming!" The door opened, and a few men dressed in pressed khaki pants and khaki shirts came out. One of them was the little girl's father. She raced up and leaped into her daddy's arms, yelling, "Daddy! Daddy! Daddy!"

Other men came out and were met with tears and warm embraces. In the past, I had thought that prison inmates were the worst people imaginable: murderers, rapists, thieves, gangsters...monsters. But now, as we stood watching families reunited, I realized that these men were not monsters. Standing before me were fathers, brothers, husbands, and sons. It's amazing what happens to you when the unexpected hits so close to home.

Finally Christopher came in, his teeth gleaming in an ear-to-ear grin. He reached out and gave his dad and me a big hug. He obviously had been eating well and had filled out—looking more like himself than I had seen him look in a long time. He had put on almost twenty pounds in four months. Now that he was working out, eating three meals a day, and sleeping regularly, his body was regaining some of the muscle he had lost from doing drugs. He looked like a brand-new person.

We sat, and Christopher told us about Lexington and how it was much better than the places he had been before. He explained that his previous stays had been in jails for people waiting to be sentenced or who had short sentences. But prisons, like Lexington, were for people with longer sentences. Prisons had many more advantages than jails did, such as a cafeteria, a recreation yard, a chapel, a library, a hobby crafts shop, and more. After Christopher had spent so many weeks in Atlanta, it sounded like he was actually happy to be here.

He also explained that they were all required to have a job. Each inmate had to first work in food service for three months, but because of Christopher's HIV status, he was exempt from working in the kitchen. Although we knew that the chance of Christopher contaminating food was slim to none, he didn't complain because many of his friends had to report to the kitchen before five o'clock each morning. Instead, he worked as a clerk in the plumbing shop. He enjoyed the chance to be busy and to get out of his unit each day. The daily schedule helped make the time go by faster, he said.

We went to the vending machines and got whatever Christopher wanted. Even though the food wasn't the healthiest, it had some variety, which Christopher didn't have in the prison cafeteria. We had sent Christopher some money, and he was able to purchase things from the prison commissary. For many inmates this was a luxury.

Before arriving, I was afraid we wouldn't have enough things to talk about to take up a six-and-a-half-hour visit. But there were so many things for us to catch up on. Besides Christopher telling us about Lexington, we filled him in on our lives at home and the office and our small group at church and Bible Study Fellowship. Before we knew it, the day had flown by.

"Thirty minutes!" The guard called out the warning.

There was something I wanted to ask Christopher before we left. I turned to him, uncertain of how to start. "You know, these past few years, Dad and I have done a lot of growing and examining ourselves and our pasts. It hasn't been easy, but I've been looking at things that have happened to me since I was a little girl. Dad and I have been working through things in our marriage. And I've also been recalling and evaluating all my years as a mother. I want to improve, and the only way that I can improve is if I know my weaknesses and my mistakes."

Christopher seemed a little surprised by what I was saying. I went ahead. "Anyway, I've done a lot of thinking and praying, and God has brought to light several things. Dad has also given me help in seeing some of my blind spots...but I want to ask for your help." I looked at my son and put my hand on his arm. "I'd really like to know... What could I have done in the past that would have helped when you were growing up? How could I have been a better mother?"

I let those words settle. I knew this was highly atypical for any Chinese parent, but I felt like this was a big part of my healing process. I wanted Christopher to be real and transparent with me.

He thought about it for a few moments and then answered, "When I was growing up—and even during my difficult years—I would have liked it if you had listened more to my heart than to my words."

Leon and I sat in silence just processing what Christopher said. It was a statement laden with such meaning. Often, as parents, Leon and I would be quick to react. We would hear Christopher's harsh words or see his bad attitude, and we would react to the situation without trying to understand what was really going on beneath the surface. Sometimes our children use words or a tone that communicates something completely different from what they are struggling with inside—whether it's fear or insecurity or pain. I realized this was a great lesson for me to learn and something that could be applied to all my relationships.

"Five minutes until visiting hours are over," the guard called out.

It was almost three o'clock. *Where did the time go?*

As the families and friends around us started saying good-bye, we saw the excitement of the morning turn to crushing sadness. Many of these men would not see their families for at least another year. The little girl who was clinging to her father's neck would be inches taller next time she saw Daddy. Tears slipped from her mother's eyes as she pried her daughter's fingers from her father's arms—it was hard to tell who was holding on more tightly, father or daughter.

"So…am I going to see you on April 10?" Christopher asked, to confirm the date we had planned out earlier.

"Of course, Christopher. We'll be here."

We shared hugs and shed a few tears as we said good-bye. Saying good-bye was never easy, especially when I was beginning to feel the years of separation between us melt away. But the realization that we would see each other in one month—not to mention all the phone calls—made the good-bye much easier.

I still wondered where Christopher was spiritually, where he was with his relationship with Christ, where he was in surrendering everything to God—including his sexuality. Leon and I could see external changes, but what was going on internally?

I was glad that Christopher was no longer doing drugs and that our relationship was much closer. But I had prayed specifically that God would do whatever it took to bring my son to him—not to us, not out of drugs, not out of homosexuality…but to the Father.

Three years earlier, I had told the dean of the dental school in Louisville that it wasn't important that Christopher became a dentist, that it was more important that Christopher became a Christ follower. I even stood on the witness stand at Christopher's sentencing hearing and told the judge not to give my son a short sentence but not to give him a long sentence either. I asked the judge to give Christopher a sentence just long enough so that our son would surrender his life to God.

And now, having settled in at the Lexington prison, was Christopher beginning that journey?

This photo shows the three of us in the visiting room the first time we saw Christopher at FMC Lexington on March 14, 1999.

These were things that Leon and I had been wondering about for months, since the start of Christopher's incarceration—and especially these past few days leading up to this visit. But we resolved to leave it all in the hands of our loving Father, and I was okay with that.

As we walked toward the exit, Christopher looked back at us and said, "Hey, Mom, Dad. I'll be standing at a window on the third floor of my unit, so look for me when you're in the parking lot. I'll be waving."

When we reached our car, we searched between the bare tree branches and squinted in the late-afternoon sun, scanning the windows on the third floor. At last, Leon caught a glimpse of some movement in a window. He pointed to it. A white T-shirt waved back and forth, and Leon and I waved back.

As we got in the car and looked behind us, the shirt continued to wave. It kept waving and waving—like a white flag of surrender, like a bright beacon of hope.

Twenty-Six

Making It Through

Christopher: June 1999

There must have been fifty inmates gathered near the Bluegrass Unit's only exit. In a few minutes it would be time for controlled movement, when we had ten minutes to move from place to place. Above the clamor, a friend called out, "Hey, Chris, you goin' to gospel choir?" Word had gotten out that I knew how to play the piano. So the guys at church talked me into joining the gospel choir.

"No," I called back. "Headed to a doctor's appointment. Can you tell Brian I won't be there?"

I hated to miss choir practice. It was one of the highlights of the week. Of the thirty or so members, most were African American. I had been in choirs before, but none of them were like this. This was real talent—raw talent. I don't know if any of the guys ever had any real training; most couldn't read music. But could they sing! It was inspiring just to be a part of this group.

But not today. The infectious-disease doctor was here, so I was headed to the hospital for a checkup and to get my blood-test results.

The front foyer continued to fill with people as we waited for the clock to hit ten before the hour. The guard sat at his desk in the middle of the foyer, not even looking up from his newspaper. Although controlled movement was scheduled at ten till the top of the hour, it technically began and ended when Control said so. The minute hand on the clock hit ten till, and I felt the crowd press closer to the door, everyone anxious to burst into the open. We were restless, looking back and forth from the clock to the guard. Finally, his walkie-talkie crackled to life. A scratchy voice spoke through the speaker: "Begin ten-minute movement! Begin ten-minute movement!"

The guard stood up and, never even looking at the inmates, fumbled for the key on his enormous key ring and unlocked the door. "Movement!" he yelled in an authoritative tone, as if we hadn't just heard it ourselves. He swung the door open and got out of the way as inmates filed through the door as quickly as possible—being careful to keep it to a fast-paced walk, since running was not allowed.

The walkways swarmed with inmates striding purposefully in every direction. A few carried empty mesh laundry bags and were headed to the store with their commissary lists—toothpaste, soap, peanut butter, canned tuna, Tupperware dishes, maybe even a radio or a set of headphones, and, of course, the staple of inmates: mackerel and ramen noodles.

Headed in the other direction were inmates with full laundry bags. They were the envy of the compound, having been to the commissary the previous hour and now trekking back to their units with their treasures. A young guy walked past with a pint of ice cream wrapped in layers of toilet paper to keep it insulated for hours.

A couple of Hispanic guys carried between them a bucket filled with ice and soda cans. They were going to sell ice-cold pop to the guys in the rec area, swapping a can of soda for a couple of thirty-three-cent, first-class stamps—each worth twenty-five cents in inmate currency on the black market. The case probably cost them thirty-six stamps, and they'd sell each of the twenty-four cans for two stamps. A three-dollar profit per case may not seem like a lot of money, but it wasn't bad in a world where fifteen cents an hour was the typical wage.

Soda selling was just one of many "hustles" going on. As they said there, "Everybody's got a hustle." I was fortunate enough to make almost thirty cents an hour at my customer-service job at UNICOR—federal prison industries. I got this job after my ninety days of working in the plumbing shop were up. But the men making twelve to seventeen cents an hour—most of the inmates—barely had enough to buy basics at the commissary. They could afford soap, shampoo, a toothbrush, and toothpaste. But if they wanted a pair of tennis shoes or a sweatshirt for twenty or thirty dollars, it was almost impossible to save up enough—unless you had a hustle.

Before I got my UNICOR job, my parents sent me money when I needed it, but I was definitely in the minority. Most men didn't have family who could or wanted to send in money. If you needed anything more than necessities, you had a hustle. Some guys did laundry—clothes washed, folded, and ironed for four stamps per load. They did great work. You'd find your T-shirts, underwear, socks, and sweats lying on your bunk in perfectly flat, perfectly even piles. Other guys would clean your room and make your bed every day. There was one guy who sold enchiladas he made from crushed corn chips. They were surprisingly good—especially to men whose daily meals were sometimes barely edible. And there were, of course, more illicit hustles, like selling food stolen from the kitchen or selling hooch and drugs. Fortunately, I was able to steer clear of drugs—and even better, I didn't miss them!

Walking from Bluegrass Unit to the hospital didn't take the full ten minutes. The real stress was the metal detector. Everybody going through the main building had to go through it. That meant long lines most of the time. And anybody standing in line who didn't get through the metal detector before the end of movement was out of luck. You were locked out and subject to punishment. It was extremely important, therefore, to be ready when it was your turn: boots off, pockets emptied. Anybody who held up the line would receive rough justice from fellow inmates who were forced to wait.

I passed by waiting rooms on the way to the infectious disease—or ID—clinic. It was the normal "hurry up and wait" routine. No one ever liked to visit the hospital, but most made the best of it and would talk with other inmates in the room. Not so at the ID clinic; the waiting room was filled with the kind of awkward silence communicating that no one wanted to be known.

There were twenty or so chairs for a handful of patients. I took a seat in an empty corner. We sat as far away from one another as possible, and nobody made eye contact. Nobody discussed his condition. Everybody knew why the others were there: either HIV or hepatitis C. If you had HIV, you didn't want others to know. News spread quickly on the prison grapevine. So in the waiting room, it was better to pretend you didn't recognize anybody else—and hope they would do the same.

One guy's body showed lipodystrophy, a side effect of HIV medication that caused a patient to have sunken cheeks, a hump back, and a bulging stomach. Another inmate's skin had turned a sickly shade of yellow brown as a result of liver failure. A male-to-female transgendered inmate, well-known on the compound, sat in the corner across from me twirling a piece of gum that stretched from her mouth. Her arms were covered with scars. I couldn't help sneaking glances at these men, wondering if I was looking at my own future—wondering how long it would be before I ended up like them.

Time dragged as I waited. I couldn't help but feel like I was in the sterile, institutionalized clinic from *One Flew Over the Cuckoo's Nest*. The building was more than sixty years old, and except for several slapped-on layers of paint, it seemed that nothing about it had been updated since it was built. Unlike other waiting rooms, it had no magazines to read, no plants to cheer up a dreary corner, no inspiring art or posters on the walls. It was simply a place to wait, and I was used to that.

I still hadn't been called when the next ten-minute movement started. That meant I would be in the hospital for at least another hour, and there was no guarantee my checkup would be finished in time for the next movement after this one. *Hurry up and wait.*

At last the doctor opened the door, looked at his clipboard, and read, "49311-019." In situations like this, I didn't regret being a number.

I followed him into the next room and sat on an exam table. The doctor looked at the sheet on his clipboard, then up at me, then back at his clipboard. "Your levels aren't looking too bad," he said. "White blood cells are pretty close to normal: CD4 count is 708. Eight hundred to twelve hundred's normal." He was very efficient but not especially friendly.

"As for your viral load," the doctor continued, "it's never going to be zero, but it's not too bad: 6,450." He rubbed his chin like he was thinking through a problem.

"Listen, uh"—he had to look down at the clipboard to get my name—"Yuan. You're healthy enough that you can choose whether to go on meds or to wait."

"Well, actually, my mom's been doing some research for me," I said. "She's contacted a few HIV specialists and sent them my numbers. Many of them recommend that at this point I can wait." Mom had told me what the doctors said to her—a few years ago, they would have automatically done an aggressive routine of meds, but those meds were pretty rough—sometimes worse than the disease. I was lucky to have a choice.

The doctor nodded.

"So my parents and I have talked it over, and we would like to wait."

"That's fine," the doctor said. "But you've got to stay on top of these blood tests. Every three months. Don't miss a doctor's appointment here."

I nodded, thinking to myself, *Where am I going to go?*

He kept his eyes on the clipboard. Not looking up, he said, "I'm sure…um…I'm sure you already know this…but um…it's my job to say it anyway…because I know things happen here in prison." He looked a little uneasy and embarrassed. He finally looked at me and blurted out, "No unsafe sex, okay? And don't share needles."

"Right. Got it," I said, trying not to laugh.

It wasn't the Mayo Clinic, but at least it was medical care. Still, these were pretty significant decisions, and I was thankful my mom had been doing so much research for me.

I exited the exam area and glanced at the clock in the waiting room. Ten minutes until movement. I sat down, avoiding the eyes of other patients, and waited, hoping we were making the right choice.

Twenty-Seven

Going to Court for the Right Reasons?

Angela: August 8, 1999

Mom, they're going to ship me out tomorrow morning. I've already packed all my stuff."

"What?" I asked, surprised at this unexpected news. "But you're not up for a transfer to a prison camp, are you? Where are you going?"

"I don't know," Christopher answered. "You know, the guards never say. But for sure, I'm coming back to Lexington because they put all my stuff in storage, so it's not going with me, which means it's not a transfer. But I have a feeling that I'm going to New York."

"New York? To help on the Kareem Abbas case? But just last week, you were telling Dad and me about how unlikely it was that they'd be using you."

Several months had passed since hearing from any agent or lawyer, so Christopher gave up hope that his sentence would be reduced in exchange for his cooperation in Abbas's trial. But regardless of whether he had to serve six years or a shorter sentence, what I wanted more than anything was for Christopher to fully surrender his life to Christ. I didn't want to put a timetable on that. But it sounded like Christopher might be going to New York after all.

"Yeah, I know," Christopher said. "Unbelievable, isn't it? I guess that's just how God works. He's really got a sense of humor, doesn't he?"

I wasn't used to Christopher talking about God so much—and so naturally. Each time he mentioned God, it was almost a shock. Only eight months earlier he was still expressing complete and utter animosity toward God and Christianity. Eight months! I could hardly believe it.

"Anyway, I just wanted to let you know that I probably won't be able to call you guys for a few days," Christopher said. "I have no idea which holdover facility I'll be in—most likely passing through Oklahoma City. But I'll call you as soon as I can. Love you."

As I hung up the phone, I thought about Christopher's growing interest in God. Although I was happy about his openness to God, I was anxious about his intentions for going to New York. Was he doing it only because he thought it would help reduce his sentence? A pastor had mentioned to me that once Christopher turned his life completely over to God, he would be out in no time. I just wanted Christopher's goal to be personal revival, not a shorter sentence.

Only time would tell.

Twenty-Eight

Snitch or Star Witness?

Christopher: August 12, 1999

G ive me your right hand." A guard rolled my fingertips from one side of the fingernail to the other over a smooth piece of wood covered with ink, then transferred that ink to a fingerprint card. He finished by putting my fingers together and pressing them down for a flat impression at the bottom of the card.

This had become old hat for me, being processed through R&D—the paperwork, strip search, more paperwork, interview, even more paperwork, and fingerprints. But sitting in a holding cell—or what we called the bull pen—for several hours at the Metropolitan Detention Center in Brooklyn would never be added to my list of favorite things to do.

On my way to Brooklyn, I spent two nights in Oklahoma City and one short night in the hated USP Atlanta. By now I was almost considered a prison veteran. Even though I had been incarcerated for only eight months, guys who were just starting their time came to me asking what prison life was like. I didn't mind sharing what to expect, but when they began asking where I was going, things got a little complicated.

The problem was that the two worst kinds of people in the prison social structure were snitches and child molesters. Anyone who cooperated with the government was a rat and was despised above all else. What concerned me was that I was heading to New York to do just that—to help convict Abbas. I had heard stories of what happened to informants, and I didn't want to meet their fate. So I told no one where I thought I was going.

When Con Air finally landed at LaGuardia, I knew my premonition was correct. I was excited about the possibility of getting out of prison sooner, but how was I going to explain to other inmates why I was in New York?

"Come on, get up. Let's go," yelled the guard, as a small group of inmates headed out of the bull pen with hands cuffed and feet shackled.

We were brought in elevators to the fifth floor, then moved to a cellblock on the north side. A guard radioed another guard inside to open the door. As we were taken through the door, I realized that this cellblock was nothing like the Atlanta City Detention Center. It wasn't a cellblock at all—because there were no cells. It was just one huge room, like a large military barracks, with one hundred or more bunks and lockers spread out. On one side of the room were a row of toilets and shower stalls—all out in the open. *This will take some getting used to,* I thought.

The guard handed me bed sheets and a pillowcase, then brought me to my bed—top bunk, of course. New guys always got the top bunk. Regardless, I was glad to see a real mattress with actual springs—like the ones we had at Lexington. I quickly made up my bed because I had one thing on my mind. Sleep.

I lay down exhausted and ready to rest, but then I heard the sound of men singing and clapping in the back corner of the pod. I pulled the pillow over my head. *Not now. Not tonight.* The singing got louder and louder, and the thin pillow did little to drown out the noise. I threw it to the side and propped myself up on one elbow. As I listened more closely, I realized they were singing in Spanish. Why were a bunch of Latinos singing at eight at night?

It was obvious that I wouldn't be getting any sleep with this commotion going on, so I looked to see what these guys were up to. They were inside a closed classroom in the far corner of the block. I could see through the windows that the men inside were clapping and raising their hands.

I got off my bed, walked across the pod, and stood by the door, looking through the small window. *Church?* I hardly understood a word they were singing, but someone inside saw me and motioned for me to come in. I slipped through the door and stood in the back.

Everyone I saw was Hispanic. There were maybe forty guys, and I felt a little out of place. I continued to listen to the songs, picking up a couple of words here or there—*Dios, Señor.* They finished singing, and an inmate in front stood up to make a few remarks in Spanish, then gestured toward me.

"Welcome," he said. His New York accent was unmistakable. "We're glad you're here." The other men looked in my direction, smiling and nodding their heads.

"I've been thinking about making our services bilingual," he continued. "So tonight, we're going to start translating our services into English." He spoke in Spanish to the rest of the group, and several men began clapping and responding with a loud, "Amennnn!"

He preached a passionate sermon, and after he finished he came over to introduce himself. His name was Eddy Mendoza. Eddy and his younger brother, Herman, were inmates and led the services each night at 5 North. They brought me over to their locker, where they had some stuff for me. They told me whenever guys first came to the unit, the church—this group of guys at 5 North—would give stuff to the new guys to help them get situated: shower slippers, toothbrush, toothpaste, and soap. It was a welcome gift. And it was the first time I had been treated like this by another group of inmates.

As I lay in bed after a shower, I thought about my new setting and the people I'd just met. I certainly didn't expect this. It was a totally different environment, and normally I'd experience anxiety over being in an unknown setting. But I felt like Eddy and Herman were guys I could get along with. Maybe things here wouldn't be so bad. And more important, nobody asked why I was here. I hoped it would stay that way.

— — —

Eddy was a passionate preacher who lived out his faith, which was evident in his reputation on the pod. Both Christian and non-Christian inmates in 5 North looked up to him and respected him. I began to spend more time with Eddy and Herman. Their sincere faith and compassion for others intrigued me.

Eddy made sure to keep the supplies for newcomers replenished, so our tithe during our services would be to donate new toothbrushes, toothpaste, soap, and shower slippers. Eddy was also a man of prayer, praying for hours each morning. He had a list of prayer requests from our little fellowship, and he prayed for our court cases, for our families, for other guys in our pod, and for guys in the pod next to us.

One night in October, I was standing by Eddy's bunk after the two of us had finished praying. He turned to me but hesitated, as if he was trying to find the right words.

"Chris," he said, "can I ask you something?"

I was a little afraid of what he was going to ask. So far no one had asked me why I was in New York. Trying to hide my concern, I answered, "Sure, what's up?"

"Have you ever thought about being a preacher or a minister?"

It was an odd question. "A preacher or a minister?" I asked.

"Yeah, well, you've only been on this pod for a couple of months, and I've seen a lot of guys come and go through this place. But I've got this feeling—well, more than just a feeling—that you'll be a minister one day."

I laughed. "Me? A minister? Yeah, right. I don't think so."

"No, really, I'm serious. I believe that one day you'll be a preacher." Eddy said it with a little more emphasis.

I continued to chuckle—the uncomfortable chuckle that comes when you don't know what to say.

"I mean it," he said. "In fact, I want you to preach this week. Bring a message from the Word for the brothers."

"Preach? This week?" I looked at Eddy, and he wasn't smiling. "You really are serious, aren't you?"

"Yeah," Eddy said. "So?"

Eddy had to be crazy. Maybe all those hours praying and fasting had gotten to his brain. "Let me pray about it," I said. That was my way of saying no—politely.

I had no real intention of preaching, nor did I think seriously about being a minister. But that night I couldn't sleep. As I tossed and turned, I thought about what Eddy had said. There was no way I could be a preacher, but I could give a little talk. I could talk on something like forgiveness, since that was something I had struggled with and something that many of these guys struggled with. A few passages from the Bible came to mind, and I got up to write them down. Before I knew it, I was scribbling down an outline and some Scripture references. As sleep finally began to overcome me, a thought lingered in my mind: *Maybe being a minister isn't so far-fetched.*

— — —

In November, I was moved from MDC Brooklyn to the Metropolitan Correctional Center in Manhattan. I had developed a great friendship with Eddy and Herman Mendoza and had begun to preach once a week at the services on 5 North. Because I was studying the Scriptures more in depth for the messages I delivered, I was growing much more in my knowledge of God. I sensed that I was growing spiritually. So obviously, I didn't want to leave 5 North. But inmates never had any say in where they were sent.

MCC Manhattan was a much older building, consisting of two-man cells. One night after the 10 p.m. count, my cellmate asked if I wanted to play a game. I wasn't sure how to respond. He turned out the lights, holding a shower slipper in his hand. I watched him in the light that came through the small window of our cell door. Seconds passed and it was all quiet—except for a mysterious clicking sound. It got faster and louder, as if it were multiplying. *What is that?*

Suddenly the lights flashed on, and my cellmate jumped to the floor, slapping at the ground with the slippers. "Gotcha!" he yelled, as he slapped the ground again and again.

I looked to my feet. Cockroaches. Everywhere. There were smashed cockroaches all over the floor and live cockroaches trying to scurry away. My cellmate was attempting to kill as many as he could before they disappeared—escaping back into the walls and behind our lockers. But it wouldn't be long before they'd be back again. I had learned that when I slept, I had to make sure the bed was pulled away from the wall and the sheets didn't touch the ground, or else I would have "friends" joining me. This was my new reality at MCC Manhattan.

— — —

One morning I made my way down to the common area. Groups of guys sat together around the pod: Hispanics over here, African Americans over there, whites here, and Chinese there. A hard, keen-eyed Chinese man spotted me across the room and nodded. I'd become somewhat of a friend to this Bruce Lee–type. He was very strong and intimidating. He had an unforgettable dragon tattoo inked into his skin. The dragon's head started on his arm with the rest of the dragon's body wrapping across his shoulder and down his back and leg, with the forked tail curling around his ankle.

There were a lot of Chinese gangsters at MCC Manhattan. Not Chinese American like me, but from mainland China. Most of them knew little English, and it had been a long time since I had spoken any Mandarin. But with little else to do and plenty to gain from being on their good side, I brushed up on my Chinese.

Before long, a guy who had just arrived on the cellblock meandered into the common room. He had dark black skin, and his hair was in tight cornrows. He was tall and thin and tried to look tough. He strutted across the room straight to the television and changed the channel. Unfortunately for him, he didn't know prison rules—one of them being you never changed the television channel when others were watching it. To make matters worse, this was the television the Chinese watched.

I knew there was going to be trouble, so I walked away. Surprisingly, so did my Chinese friends. Was this guy going to escape the consequence of his stupid actions? But before I even reached the steps, one of the Chinese guys turned back with a small pair of scissors in his hands—sharpened like razors. In a split second he cut the young perpetrator from head to foot. It wasn't a pretty sight. Some people had to learn the hard way.

— — —

I'd made some friends in Manhattan, but I still missed the Mendoza brothers. There was no large group of Christians in this cellblock, only a half-dozen guys who met every night without a leader. Fortunately, I still had the notes from the messages I gave on 5 North. So I recycled them and began to lead services each night.

Since our group was small, I wouldn't call what I did preaching—maybe more like leading a Bible study. Nevertheless, I spent much of my days preparing. But without any training on how to read the Bible or lead a Bible study, I sometimes felt like we were the blind leading the blind. And yet, the guys encouraged me, and our little fellowship grew.

Sometimes when new people came to the cellblock, they would come to our gathering, looking like deer caught in the headlights. We didn't have any welcome kits to give them, but I tried to spend time with them to help them get adjusted. Often, I had the opportunity to share the gospel with them—and amazingly, many of them made decisions to follow Christ. I actually began to enjoy being a part of God's work on this block, and I couldn't stop thinking about what Eddy had said about me. As crazy as it seemed, maybe there was some truth to it.

— — —

The February wind whipped through the streets of New York as I was transported to the federal courthouse. The day had come for me to testify against Kareem Abbas. Six months had passed since I arrived in New York. I had spent the first couple of months with federal agents going through all my records—the ones they had confiscated from my filing cabinet in Atlanta two years prior. Then we took a break until a few weeks before the trial, when we spent time preparing for me to be on the witness stand. The assistant U.S. attorney prosecuting Abbas had taken several of my records and enlarged them for display on a large poster board to be used as exhibits during the trial. I was the first witness to be questioned.

I climbed up to the witness stand and saw Kareem glaring at me. I knew he would be angry, but I remembered Ephesians 5:11: "Have nothing to do with the fruitless deeds of darkness, but rather expose them."

I was there to shed light, to make things visible. *Who knows?* I thought. *Prison could turn out for the better for Kareem. If not for prison, I would probably be dead now.* I believed that God had used prison to literally save my life.

I was sworn in, then sat back as lawyers started going over the evidence. It was clear that Kareem didn't have much of a chance. They had confiscated too much evidence from my filing cabinet. Everything was in black and white. Whole pages of my daily planner and ledger were used as court exhibits, revealing exactly when, what, and how much I had bought from Kareem Abbas.

As Abbas's lawyer came forward for cross-examination, a wave of nervousness swept over me. This was the first time I'd been on a witness stand. He pulled out some pages from my daily planner and began asking questions.

"According to your records, it says that you bought some ketamine, Ecstasy, and ice from Mr. Abbas here in New York on June 18, 1997? Is that correct?"

"Yes, that's correct."

"Well, then. How do you explain the fact that your daily planner does not show any record that you were in New York? In fact, on these dates around June 18, it shows that you had appointments and activities all back in Atlanta. But nothing in New York. How do you explain this?"

My heart skipped a beat. We had practiced this for hours; I knew these dates and times by heart. I was certain that I was right. I was in New York on June 18 to buy from Kareem. I scanned the daily-planner page again, which Abbas's attorney held up for the jury to see. A smug smile spread across his face. But then I noticed something in the corner of the poster.

I looked at the attorney and said, "Well, sir, with all due respect…if you look in the upper left-hand corner, that page from my daily planner is not from 1997; it's from 1996. That's why it doesn't match up with the prosecution's account of what Kareem and I were doing."

The lawyer's mouth formed a hard, straight line, and a vein popped out on his forehead. He stared at me, then gave the judge an embarrassed look. "I have no more questions," he said.

I was told that the trial went on for another week with other inmate witnesses who were cooperating with the government. In the end, Abbas was found guilty. It was a strange feeling to have received that news. I no longer held a grudge against him for how he had ripped me off. Rather, I hoped that this would turn out for the better for him—as prison had turned out for the better for me.

But the best part about all of this was that I was finally leaving New York and going back to Lexington. I had to first stop through Atlanta for a reduction-in-sentence hearing, initiated by Abbas's prosecutor in light of my cooperation. I definitely didn't look forward to being back in USP Atlanta. But I hadn't seen my parents for more than six months while I was in New York, and they would be at my hearing in Atlanta. I couldn't wait to see them.

Twenty-Nine

Truly Extraordinary

Angela: April 17, 2000

L eon and I were back in a courtroom in Atlanta at the Richard B. Russell Federal Building. Just fifteen months earlier, I had sat in this courtroom and asked the judge to give Christopher not too little time and not too much time—but just enough for God to change his life.

The Kareem Abbas trial in New York was over, and Christopher had been brought to Atlanta for his reduction-in-sentence hearing. Christopher's lawyer explained to Leon and me that the chance of the judge shortening our son's sentence was slim to none. This judge seldom gave out a lesser sentence, and Christopher's prosecuting attorney, Ms. O'Brien, would not give in without a strong fight.

About a half hour earlier, we had been able to visit with Christopher through a thick glass window, and something he said still replayed in my mind: *"I'm actually okay if the judge doesn't reduce my sentence even on day. I'm content with where I am now—being here in prison."* This surprised me, but it was exactly what I'd been praying for. What he said next surprised me even more.

"Dad, Mom, I've been praying a lot lately, and I feel that God has called me into ministry. I don't know what all that means. But I've realized that it doesn't matter where I am—whether in prison or out of prison—I'm going to serve the Lord."

As I sat on a wooden bench in the courtroom, I still couldn't believe the words that had come out of Christopher's mouth. And Leon was just as surprised as I was. We had known there was a difference in Christopher; he had been teaching and leading Bible studies. Most of our time on the phone had been spent talking about what he had been studying. And we would share with him things we'd been learning in Bible Study Fellowship. Christopher often incorporated what we'd talked about over the phone into his messages on the cellblock. We'd known there was a difference, but we didn't realize to what extent…until now.

The heavy wooden doors opened and a marshal walked into the courtroom, followed by Christopher. He smiled at us as he made his way to the table on the right, next to his lawyer. Opposite them, Ms. O'Brien, the prosecuting attorney, sat on the left side of the courtroom with Ms. Peters, the prosecuting attorney from the Abbas trial in New York. Ms. Peters had flown down specifically to testify on Christopher's behalf. Our lawyer had told us that in all the years he had practiced, he'd never seen a prosecutor come from another district to vouch for an inmate witness.

As Christopher stood there, I noticed Ms. O'Brien kept looking at him. She hadn't seen Christopher since she prosecuted him fifteen months earlier, and her eyes widened as if in astonishment. Christopher was a totally different person than he'd been before—and it was evident just by his countenance.

Still, Ms. O'Brien was incredibly smart; she always spoke without notes in perfectly formed paragraphs. Her only impression of Christopher was that of an addict, a criminal, a drug dealer. She certainly had had no respect for him fifteen months ago.

The judge entered the courtroom and the hearing began. After the initial greetings, he gave Ms. O'Brien the opportunity to speak.

"Your Honor," she said, "I am going to actually turn it over to Ms. Peters, who handled the prosecution in New York, so that she can explain in more detail Mr. Yuan's cooperation."

Ms. Peters began by telling the judge that when Ms. O'Brien had described Christopher to her, Ms. Peters had doubts about using him as a witness. But after working with him, she realized this was someone completely different than the person Ms. O'Brien had first described. She said Christopher had provided valuable information and had been cooperative, trustworthy, focused, articulate, and probably her star witness. She further stated that it would have been difficult to try the case without Christopher's testimony.

"Kareem Abbas has been involved since probably the early nineties in distributing hundreds of thousands of pills. We were very fortunate when Mr. Yuan came to us," Ms. Peters concluded.

Next, it was Christopher's lawyer's turn to speak. He stood up and pointed at our son. "The person who stands before you today is, in fact, a different person from the one who stood before you on January 9, 1999— the one you sentenced to seventy-two months of incarceration. If Your Honor pleases, his mother is here and would like to address you in that regard."

The judge nodded, and I was called to the stand. I stood slowly, my knees weak at the opportunity to speak in support of my son and to testify about God's grace. I fumbled with the edges of the paper in my hands as I approached the witness stand and sat down.

"Will you tell the court who you are, please?"

"I'm Angela Yuan, mother of Christopher Yuan." I met Leon's gaze, and I found the courage to say everything I'd prepared. I told the court that I represented my entire family in speaking about the change in Christopher's life. I told of my prayers for God to turn Christopher's life around and about the conversations we'd had, the Bible study Christopher was leading in prison, and the leadership role he had taken among his fellow inmates. And I explained that I had seen wisdom and understanding in Christopher, where before I'd seen only loss and confusion.

But that's not all I had to say to the judge. I turned to him and said, "Thank you for the sentence you gave to Christopher a year ago. We have seen the positive impact it has had on him. Thank you, Your Honor."

The judge seemed surprised by my last words. I stepped down from the stand and took a deep breath, glad to have accomplished what I wanted to say. I returned to my seat, where Leon smiled and patted my hand. I looked toward Christopher, and he nodded his appreciation. *Please, God,* I prayed, *not my will, but your will be done.*

Ms. Peters had made it easy for Christopher's attorney, who only had to summarize the federal prosecutor's words before he made a bold plea for the judge to shorten Christopher's sentence to thirty-six months. *Thirty-six months,* I thought. *That's half! Pretty optimistic.*

The judge looked to Ms. O'Brien to rebut, but she declined. We could see the surprise in Christopher's face when Ms. O'Brien took her seat, not arguing to keep his sentence as it was.

The judge looked over his papers and then fixed his gaze on Christopher. He informed us that in order for there to be a sentence reduction, there must be more than just cooperation involved. He only shortened sentences when the cooperation has been truly extraordinary. He paused and took off his glasses, setting them on his desk.

"I believe that there has been such a showing in this case," the judge said. "I'll grant the motion for a reduction in sentence, and I'll resentence Mr. Yuan to a term of thirty-six months in the custody of the Bureau of Prisons."

Thirty-six months! That's three years! I couldn't believe it. It wouldn't be long before our son would be released…and Christopher would be coming home.

Thirty

Holy Sexuality

Christopher: September 2000

The low rumble of voices that usually echoed through Bluegrass Unit at the Federal Medical Center in Lexington was silenced every afternoon for the 4 p.m. stand-up count. It meant we had to stand by our assigned bunks and be counted by the guards. It also meant that while we waited for count to clear, we had to be quiet. Often guys complained about the interruption to their day—it brought them back in from the yard, away from watching television or hanging out with friends. But I actually didn't mind. It was peace and quiet—a precious commodity in prison—and it gave me time to sit on my bunk and think.

I had been locked up a total of twenty-one months. I had fifteen months to go until my full sentence was technically done. But because of good time, five months were knocked off my sentence. With only ten months left, I was going to be transferred to a prison camp in Illinois and then to a halfway house in Chicago.[18] I couldn't believe I was getting out of prison so soon...and going home.

It almost sounded weird to think that going back to Chicago was going home. But it was. It definitely was the last thing I would have thought three years earlier when I was living in Atlanta, or even twenty-one months ago when I was first locked up. But a lot had changed since then—a whole lot.

I looked at the Bible that lay beside me. That, for one, was a huge change. I would never have picked up that book two years earlier. But now, here I was studying it and even teaching it! It was almost funny. The interesting thing was, even when I was selling drugs, I believed in God. But it was my own idea of God. In prison, after reading the Bible, I came across James 2:19 (NASB), which said, "Demons also believe, and shudder." I realized that simply believing was not enough.

The more I studied the Bible, the more I learned that loving God was not how I felt or what I thought. In the New Testament, I read these words: "We know that we have come to know him if we obey his commands," and, "This is love for God: to obey his commands" (1 John 2:3; 5:3). Knowing and loving God, both, are all about obedience. Before, I had thought I was a pretty good person. Sure, I had been selling drugs and taking drugs. But when I was at the Atlanta City Detention Center and not doing drugs, I still wanted to take drugs. I craved them. And later, when I gave my life to Christ, I realized that I had made drugs my idol.

Idolatry isn't simply worshiping a carved image; an idol is the one thing I think I can't live without. For me, that was drugs.

Because of my past drug use, I was required to participate in Alcoholics Anonymous and Narcotics Anonymous meetings at the Lexington prison, and one of the twelve steps is to make a "searching and fearless moral inventory of ourselves." When I did that, the most obvious of all the idols I had in my life was drugs.

But within a few months of my incarceration, I no longer craved ice or Ecstasy. I no longer dreamed about getting high. I no longer smelled or tasted meth throughout the day. I believed that God simply and yet miraculously took it all away. And yet, I knew that this was very unusual, since most of my friends continued to struggle long after their last hit. But for some reason, the pull was no longer there for me—maybe it was because there were other idols that God wanted me to deal with.

One of those idols had been my love for dance music and the glamour of nightlife. While music and clubs weren't necessarily sins in themselves, my days were often consumed by thinking about them. When I bought a radio at the prison commissary in Atlanta—and later in Lexington—the first thing I did was find the stations that played dance music. The music pulled me back to the years when I lived for going to clubs, and I reminisced about the fame, the glamour, the "bling-bling." I started to think I'd be able to go back to the clubs after I got out of prison. But nightclubs could too easily lead me back to drugs—and I didn't want that.

So I had asked myself the question, *Can I live without the music, without the clubs?* It was a hard question to answer, and I decided to try to fast from listening to music and try not to dwell on the nightlife. At first, it was really hard. But eventually it got easier, and finally it was quite liberating. I didn't need it after all. I could live without the music, the clubs, and the glamour.

I heard the jangling of keys and the turning of the lock. The huge metal door down the hall opened. "Count!" bellowed the guard. I stood next to my bunk, as did my three roommates. The *clap-clap* of work boots striking the concrete floor neared our room. There were always two guards. We joked that they needed two guards so they'd have enough fingers to count the inmates in one hallway. After they passed, we got back up in our beds and waited for Control to announce that count had cleared—or for a recount and do it all over again. Count lasted anywhere from forty-five minutes to an hour and a half—plenty of time for me to sit and think.

I was continuing a personal inventory. *What other idols are in my life? What else do I think I can't live without?* I had asked myself this question periodically for a year and a half. There were several things that God had convicted me of, but it seemed that I was holding on to one last thing. And that was sex. I had an addiction to sex. Having several anonymous partners at a bathhouse in the same day had been nothing out of the ordinary for me.

But could I now live without sex? Was that even possible?

To live without sex—especially in light of my past life—was difficult to even think about. In the past, I always figured that just as I needed food and water, I needed sex. God wouldn't anymore ask me to give up sex than he would ask me to give up eating or sleeping—or so I thought.

But the reality was that for the past two years, I hadn't been as sexually active as I had been outside of prison. I had gone days, weeks, and even months without sex—and survived! I hadn't developed any irreversible side effects. It wasn't cruel and unusual punishment. Abstinence was not an unreasonable or impossible thing. And as I read through the Bible, I realized there were people who lived their whole lives without sex, like Jesus—yet he was complete and whole. Paul was also single and spoke positively about singleness, sexual purity, and abstinence. Maybe I had made sex an idol. Maybe living without sex was not only possible, but healthy and good for me.

It was apparent that the Bible condemned my past sexual promiscuity, but I still wondered what the verdict was on homosexuality. As I continued to read the Bible, it was clear that God loved me unconditionally. But I'd also come across some passages that seemed to condemn the core of who I thought I was—my homosexuality. Being a new believer and not having any Bible training, I wanted to get someone else's opinion. So several months earlier, I had gone to a chaplain and opened up to him. I'd shared with him my past—living as a gay man and now living with HIV. I had been nervous about how the chaplain would respond. Fortunately, he had been very gracious and listened to me with compassion. Then he said something that totally surprised me.

"Actually, the Bible doesn't condemn homosexuality." He walked over to a bookshelf. "Here's a book that explains this view in more detail." He handed me the book, and I took it in the hope of finding biblical justification for homosexuality.

I sat in the chapel's small courtyard to read, with the chaplain's book in one hand and my Bible in the other. I had every reason in the world to accept the book's assertion that God was okay with my homosexuality and gay identity. If I could be a Christian and have a steady relationship with a man, that would be just about ideal. I'd go to church with him and maybe even start a family. It would be such a relief if this could all be reconciled.

But as I started reading the book and reading the Bible passages it referred to, God's Holy Spirit convicted me that the assertions from that book were a distortion of God's truth. Reading his Word, I couldn't deny his unmistakable condemnations of homosexual sex. I wasn't even able to get through the first chapter of that book, and I gave it back to the chaplain.

After that, I turned to the Bible alone and went through every verse, every chapter, every page of Scripture looking for biblical justification for homosexuality. I couldn't find any. I was at a turning point, and a decision had to be made. Either abandon God to live as a homosexual—by allowing my feelings and sexual passions to dictate who I was. Or abandon homosexuality—by liberating myself from my feelings—and live as a follower of Jesus Christ.

My decision was obvious. I chose God.

As I continued to read the Bible, I came across Leviticus 18:22 and 20:13 (NASB)—passages normally used to condemn gays and lesbians to a fiery fate. "You shall not lie with a male as one lies with a female; it is an abomination." But I realized that God didn't call *lesbians and gay men* abominations. He called *it* an abomination. What God condemned was the act, not the person. For so long, I had gotten the message from the Christian protestors at gay-pride parades that the God of the Bible hated people like me, because we were abominations. But after reading these passages, I saw that God didn't hate me; nor was he condemning me to an inescapable destiny of torment. But rather, it was the sex he condemned, and yet he still wanted an intimate relationship with me.

I had learned that I could live without sex, but what about my sexuality? If I was abandoning homosexuality as the core of who I was, did I have an identity apart from my sexual orientation? I really struggled with this, especially during my first year in prison. For the longest time, I really believed that God had created me this way—gay. I had told myself over and over, *I am gay. I was born this way. This is who I am. I never chose to have these feelings.* But now, as I searched the Scriptures for the way I should live, I began to ask myself a different question: *Who am I apart from my sexuality?* I didn't have an answer.

As I continued to read the Bible, I realized that my identity shouldn't be defined by my sexuality. Paul said in Acts 17:28, "For in him we live and move and have our being." Christ should be everything—my all in all. My sexual orientation didn't have to be the core of who I was. My primary identity didn't have to be defined by my feelings or sexual attractions. My identity was not "gay" or "homosexual," or even "heterosexual," for that matter. But my identity as a child of the living God must be in Jesus Christ alone.

God says, "Be holy, for I am holy."[19] I had always thought that the opposite of homosexuality was heterosexuality. But actually the opposite of homosexuality is holiness. God never said, "Be heterosexual, for I am heterosexual." He said, "Be holy, for I am holy."

For the longest time, I could never see myself becoming straight. It was a burden, because I felt I had to somehow become straight to please God. So when I realized that heterosexuality should not be my goal, it was so freeing. The thing was, if I did become straight, I would still deal with lust. Therefore, I knew that I shouldn't focus on homosexuality or even heterosexuality, but on the one thing that God calls everyone to: holy sexuality. Holy sexuality is not focused on orientation change—becoming straight—but on obedience. And I realized that obedience means, no matter what my situation, no matter what my feelings—gay or straight—I must obey and be faithful to God.

Holy sexuality means one of two scenarios. The first scenario is marriage. If a man is married, he must devote himself to complete faithfulness to his wife. And if a woman is married, she must devote herself to complete faithfulness to her husband. The idea that I might marry a woman had seemed like an impossibility—though God could do the impossible. But the truth was, I did not need to be attracted to women in general to get married; I needed to be attracted to only one woman. Heterosexuality is a broad term that focuses on sexual feelings and behaviors toward the opposite gender. It includes lust, adultery, and sex before marriage—all sins according to the Bible. God calls married people to something much more specific—*holy sexuality.* Holy sexuality means focusing all our sexual feelings and behaviors exclusively toward *one* person, our spouse.

The second scenario of holy sexuality is singleness. Single people must devote themselves to complete faithfulness to the Lord through celibacy. This is clearly taught throughout Scripture, and abstinence is not something unfair or unreasonable for God to ask of his people. Singleness is not a curse. Singleness is not a burden. As heirs of the new covenant, we know that the emphasis is not on procreation but regeneration.[20] But singleness need not be permanent. It merely means being content in our present situation while being open to marriage—and yet not consumed by the pursuit of marriage.

Holy sexuality doesn't mean that I no longer have any sexual feelings or attractions. Nor is it the obliteration of my sexuality either. God created us as sexual beings with the natural desire for intimacy. And everyone is created to desire intimate, God-honoring, nonsexual relationships with the same gender. But because of the effects of original sin, this normal feeling has been distorted. I believe homosexuality (and any other sin, such as jealousy, pride, and gluttony) stems from a legitimate need fulfilled in an illegitimate way.

So the question is, if I continue to have these feelings I neither asked for nor chose, will I still be willing to follow Christ no matter what? Is my obedience to Christ dependent on whether he answered my prayers my way? God's faithfulness is proved not by the elimination of hardships but by carrying us through them. Change is not the absence of struggles; change is the freedom to choose holiness in the midst of our struggles. I realized that the ultimate issue has to be that I yearn after God in total surrender and complete obedience.

I was brought back to the present when I heard the rattling of keys opening the unit's hallway door. "Count cleared!" shouted the guard. My roommates leaped out of bed and began getting ready for dinner. I sat staring at the wall as they headed to chow.

What do I think I can't live without? This was the question I had been asking. And finally, I was finding some answers. I was realizing that there were a lot of things I *could* live without—and it was freeing. I was not controlled by my past addictions, my old idols, my sexual attractions, or my sexuality.

What do I think I can't live without? Well, there was one thing, or more specifically one person, I *knew* I couldn't live without—Jesus. And I needed more and more of him each day.

Lord, you are sufficient; you are all I need...and don't let me ever, ever forget that.

Thirty-One

Redeemed

Angela: September 2000

I cradled the phone to my ear, enjoying a quick conversation with Christopher as I finished washing the dishes from dinner.

"I've been thinking and praying about what I'm going to do when I get out in July next year," he said. "I think that I'd like to go back to school. I have over two hundred hours of college and graduate-school credit—but no degree. It's time that I finally got a degree."

"What do you want to study?" I asked. "And where are you thinking about going to school?"

"Well, I've realized how little I actually know about the Bible. And if I'm going to continue in ministry, I'd better learn more about the Bible than just the religion I learned here in prison. I'm thinking about going to Bible college. Do you think you can send me some information and an application from that Bible school in Chicago called Moody Bible Institute?"

The phone slipped from my ear, dropped onto the counter, and almost fell into the sink. I grabbed the phone with soap bubbles clinging to my hand. Bible college? Moody Bible Institute? I put the phone back to my ear.

"Mom, are you there?"

"Yes, sorry. I'm here."

"What happened?"

"I dropped the phone. I'm just really surprised that you want to go to Bible college. And Moody Bible Institute? How do you know about Moody?"

"Remember whenever I came home from Louisville? You and Dad would have that Moody radio station playing on the intercom—like all day long! I think you guys did that on purpose, didn't you?"

We laughed, and I marveled that he had been paying any attention at all back then. Leon and I normally played Moody Radio for most of the day, even when Leon was seeing patients. But we specifically wanted Christopher to have a taste of Christian radio, hoping seeds might be planted—and they were! Now here I was, listening to Christopher tell me about his plans to go to Bible school after prison. I would never have dreamed this would have happened!

Leon and I called the admissions department at Moody, and they sent Christopher an application. When he got it, he began filling it out and writing the essays. But he was a little worried about the references he needed. Moody requested references from people who had known him as a Christian for at least one year. Christopher didn't have many choices in the prison at Lexington. He was finally able to persuade a prison chaplain, a prison guard, and another inmate to write references for him. I wondered how often Moody received applications like this one!

On October 5, Christopher was transferred from Lexington to the federal prison camp in Marion, Illinois. The Bureau of Prisons gave him a furlough release, which meant that he was not being escorted by marshals or taken on Con Air. He was allowed to travel in a regular, commercial airplane. I could hear the excitement in his voice when he called us.

"Hey, Mom! I'm at the Lexington airport. I went through R&D around seven, then got into a van with a guard who drove me here and just dropped me off at eight fifteen! The prison gave me ten dollars cash, so I'm calling from a regular pay phone. No collect call. No phone monitoring. But the best part is that I'm not handcuffed and shackled; I'm just walking around like everybody else! I'm beginning to feel like a human again."

"That's great, Christopher." We chatted some more, and then I asked, "So is your flight going directly to Marion?"

"No, I have a layover in St. Louis, and then I go from there to Marion. I have to report to the prison by 1:05 p.m."

I heard an announcement in the background: "Now boarding TWA Flight 4511…"

"That's my plane, Mom. I've gotta go. I'll call you when I land in St. Louis. Love you."

"Love you too, Christopher."

He called later from St. Louis and then a second time when his flight to Marion was delayed for two to three hours. I was concerned about the delay. "You're supposed to report to Marion at 1:05," I said. "Are you going to get in trouble?"

"I called them already," Christopher said. "They said it's fine. I was a little scared—what if they didn't believe me? Fortunately, they already knew about the delay. I'll have two extra hours of freedom here, and I'm enjoying every minute of it! It's great to just watch people walk by. And even better that nobody's watching me back!"

He called later from Marion and said he had eaten at a Mexican restaurant at the airport.

"How was it?" I asked, laughing again at the delight a simple plane trip brought my son.

"It was so good. They waited on me and brought me my food. What a difference from the prison cafeteria! I better be going, though. You guys still coming in a week and a half to visit?"

"You know we will."

"Good. Well, I'll call you from the camp when I get there."

"Sounds good. Love you, Christopher."

"Love you too, Mom."

Leon and I visited Christopher at the prison camp ten days later, on a Sunday. The camp was right next to an underground supermax prison facility where inmates were kept on permanent lockdown. When Alcatraz was shut down, the Federal Bureau of Prisons brought all of those inmates here to "The New Rock." But at the camp, things were much different. There was no fence, no barbed wire, no guard towers. There was only a small sign that read, *Out of Bounds.*

Christopher told us how much more freedom he had here, with no controlled movements. However, the food and programs were not as good as at Lexington, since there were fewer inmates. Fortunately, there was a gym where he lifted weights with a former pro football player named Hanz and quickly bulked up to one hundred eighty-five pounds.

Christopher's unit manager told him that if he continued with good behavior, he'd be transferred to Chicago's halfway house on February 15, 2001. Although Christopher would still be officially under the supervision of the Federal Bureau of Prisons, there was the possibility of going home on weekends or even being placed on home confinement. His official release date was still July 15, 2001, but it made February seem like an unofficial release date since he was able to transition back into society—and family life.

February was less than four months away, and Christopher was required to find a job while under the supervision of the halfway house. But the bigger question was what he was going to do after July. Christopher had filled out Moody's application, and we would probably be able to hand deliver it while visiting the campus in March. I had no idea how Moody was going to respond to Christopher's application. I only hoped that they would give our son a second chance.

— — —

The alarm clock on the hotel nightstand sounded, and Leon reached to turn it off. He tilted the clock face up: 6:00 a.m.

We were in Dallas for a missions conference called the Finishers Forum. The night before, we had arrived at the conference hall a few minutes late and ended up sitting all the way in the back. Leon and I were normally front-row people, and sitting so far back, we had to strain to see the speaker. We were determined to get a better seat for this morning's 9:00 a.m. session.

Leon got dressed and went to the banquet room at 7:00. He staked out the two best seats in the room—putting our Bibles on one of the round tables at the front. Then we took our time getting ready and headed out for a leisurely breakfast, arriving back at the session just as it was about to start. The room was almost full by the time we got there, but we could see our seats—front and center.

Shuffling through the crowd and maneuvering between tables and chairs, we finally arrived at our seats and sat down. A tall, handsome man graying around the temples sat to Leon's right. To my left were two pleasant-looking couples. We'd only been seated a moment when Leon and I looked at each other, both feeling that something wasn't quite right.

I glanced at the name tag of the woman next to me. *Marge Malwitz,* it read. *I know that name from somewhere,* I thought. Then I looked at her husband and recognized Nelson Malwitz, the founder of the Finishers Project, the organization that hosted this conference. An embarrassing realization dawned on me. We had reserved our own seats at the speakers' head table!

Leon realized our mistake at the same time I did. His eyes were wide, and he quickly gathered up his Bible and papers. "I'm so sorry," he whispered to the Malwitzes as he rose from his chair. "I didn't know this was the head table. We'll sit somewhere else."

Mrs. Malwitz put her hand on Leon's Bible. "You're fine!" she said. "Don't go anywhere. We want you here."

She introduced herself and her husband, Nelson. "And this fellow to Leon's right," Mrs. Malwitz said, "is this morning's speaker, Dr. Joe Stowell...president of Moody Bible Institute."

I had listened to Dr. Stowell for years and had heard him at countless conferences—but never had I been this close to him. I couldn't have been more stunned. Leon and I sat there speechless. Dr. Stowell smiled and nodded at us. We hadn't looked at the schedule to see who would be speaking during the conference, so we had no idea he would be here. We were sharing a table with the head of the school that Christopher was hoping to attend!

Dr. Stowell made his way to the podium and began to speak. Normally, I try to catch everything that he says, whether it's on the radio or at a conference. But this morning I didn't hear a word. My heart was racing, and my mind was filled with thoughts. I knew this was not a coincidence that we were sitting right next to Dr. Stowell—even though it was our mistake. I wanted to say something to him about Christopher. But what should I say? At this point, I couldn't come up with any words. I prayed that God would give me the exact words to speak, something short but memorable so that Dr. Stowell wouldn't forget about Christopher. I prayed and prayed through his entire message that God would give me some words to say.

I had been to enough conferences to know that there would be a long line of people wanting to talk to Dr. Stowell when he finished. From where I sat, Leon and I would obviously be first in line. But I couldn't be long with him—maybe only a minute. I didn't want to stumble over my English or say anything embarrassing.

He finished his talk and returned to his seat as the emcee made a few announcements and closed in prayer. It felt like my heart was going to jump out of my throat. I knew I had to seize this once-in-a-lifetime opportunity—but still I had no words to say. As the emcee dismissed us for a short break and I saw people beginning to make their way toward Dr. Stowell, I stammered, "Dr. Stowell...I...I have a quick question..."

"Yes"—he looked at my name tag—"Mrs. Yuan?"

"Dr. Stowell," I asked, "does...does Moody accept sinners?"

Dr. Stowell paused and gave me a perplexed look.

Taken in 2009, this photo shows Christopher and me, two prodigals redeemed.

"Well," I continued, "the reason why I ask is because my son will be coming out of prison soon. And he wants to study at Moody." I explained a bit more about Christopher's past and his current situation.

Dr. Stowell thought for a moment, then asked me a simple but profound question. "Has he been redeemed?"

A smile spread across my face, and I dropped my tense shoulders. "Yes," I said and sighed. "He has been. He has been redeemed."

Thirty-Two

Finally Home

Christopher: February 15, 2001

S ign here and date here," the officer directed, pointing to two blank lines on the page in front of me. I had been looking forward to this day for so long that I almost couldn't believe it was here. Even though this wasn't my official release date, it was the day I was transferred by furlough release to a halfway house in Chicago. This time my parents were picking me up to take me to the halfway house—but not before swinging by home. It had been so long since I'd been home, and even longer yet since I considered home to be…home.

I touched the tip of the pen to the paper, then stopped at the first line. *Name.* To everyone but my family, I had always been just Chris. But my birth name was *Christopher*—"Christ-bearer."

Here I stood on the cusp of a new life. Perhaps it was time for a new name. Or actually, perhaps it was time I reclaimed my old name. My time in prison was basically done. That evening I'd be in a new place—halfway to freedom. I was about to sign on the dotted line.

Christopher. It didn't quite feel natural. *Christopher.* Every time I heard the name, it felt a little odd. But maybe that peculiar feeling I got could be a reminder that I wasn't who I used to be. I was no longer Chris. I would be Christopher. Christ-bearer.

I tossed my canvas sea bag with my personal belongings into the white van, then climbed in the back. The guard sitting in the driver's seat turned around. "Ready?" he asked. "Okay, let's go."

The van cranked up to a steady rumble, and we headed out. We passed the chapel, the steel building where people came to visit inmates, the *Out of Bounds* sign, the supermax prison, the wardens' houses, and finally up to the guards' gatehouse. I could see my parents' Honda stopped beside the front gate. Dad and Mom were standing there waiting for me. I smiled. This was it. This was the end of my time in prison—and the beginning of a brand-new life.

When the van shuddered to a stop, I hopped out and walked straight to my parents. With tears and laughter they embraced me. My mother wrapped me in a jacket to cover the prison-issue khaki shirt. As she did, I thought of the father of the prodigal son, who ran to meet his son when he finally returned from that far country: "Quick! Bring the best robe and put it on him."[21] I pulled the coat tight around me, appreciating the warmth and love it represented.

— — —

The vast cornfields of Illinois fell away on either side of the interstate highway as we drove toward home. I had always taken the wide spaces of Illinois for granted, but now—seen through clear glass with no bars or mesh—they looked more beautiful than ever.

We spoke very little during the drive. I couldn't believe that this time was over. No more handcuffs. No more chains. No more guards. No more stand-up counts. I mostly soaked in the freedom of this new start. I could hardly put into words the gratitude I felt for God's work in my life—and for my parents, who had every reason to give up on me. But they never did.

I looked at my mother. She was leaning against the headrest, her eyes closed and a smile of contentment lit up her face. It hit me then, the significance of what they had done for me. They must have been worried day and night. They had probably dealt with criticism and condescension from people in their community. *"Oh yes, they're the ones with the son in prison."*

And the countless hours in prayer my parents had spent on my behalf. I had seen my mother's knees, brown and calloused from kneeling in her prayer closet. And the pages of my father's Bible worn from thumbing through God's promises. They'd done this for me, their son who stormed out almost eight years ago, yelling that he had a real family—his gay friends. But my real family, as it turned out, was my real family. How would I ever repay them?

I reached forward and squeezed my mom's shoulder. She turned and smiled.

"Thank you," I said, looking at both of them. "Thank you so much."

— — —

It took us almost six hours to drive to our home in the Chicago suburbs. As we drove slowly past the front of the house, I looked at the large pine tree in the yard. There was a huge yellow ribbon tied around it.

"Tie a yellow ribbon 'round the old oak tree..."[22] It had been a long time since I'd thought of that oldie. It was such a great, sentimental story about an inmate returning home. He'd asked his love to tie a ribbon around the tree in their yard if she'd still have him. And if there was no ribbon on the tree, he'd told the bus driver not to stop but to keep driving. He was afraid to open his eyes as they approached his street. Then he heard the passengers in the bus cheering because there wasn't just one ribbon but a hundred yellow ribbons around the oak tree.

As I watched the ends of the yellow ribbon moving in the breeze, it occurred to me how much my life was like that song. *"It's been three long years. Do you still want me?"* Three years ago my apartment in Atlanta was raided, and I was hauled off to jail. I was unworthy of my parents' love, but they both still wanted me and had waited for me after all this time. My eyes misted and my heart flooded with the understanding of grace and forgiveness that had been given to me. I squeezed my mother's hand.

As we approached the front door, I could hear the faint sound of singing. I looked to my parents with a bit of confusion. They just smiled—with a twinkle in their eyes—and pushed open the door. In the front hallway sat a CD player, which had been playing "Tie a Yellow Ribbon" on repeat since they'd left home yesterday morning to pick me up. They wanted it to be the first thing I heard when I came home.

I stepped into the entrance and looked around the front foyer, and I saw more than a hundred yellow ribbons tacked here and there on all the walls. I walked closer and saw each one had a signature and some words of encouragement.

"Each ribbon was signed by someone who has been praying for you all these years," my mother explained. "And they each wanted to personally welcome you home."

It was almost more than I could bear. That much love, that much perseverance, and that much grace extended by so many people, many of whom I had never met. They didn't love me simply because of who I was; they loved me because they loved Jesus. And they, like my parents, were willing to give me a second chance.

My mother embraced me, her eyes shining. "Christopher, welcome home."

"Christopher," I said, my voice choked by tears. "Christ-bearer," I whispered.

"Yes, Christopher." In that moment I realized that her journey had been just as long and painful as mine.

"I'm home, Mom. I'm home." And I knew what I said was true in every way. After being lost so long in a far country…I was finally home.

Where Are They Now?

Christopher: September 30, 2010

I t was a warm Indian summer morning as I walked to the Metra train platform. I glanced at my watch: 8:52 a.m. I could hear the rumble of the commuter train coming down the tracks. It was right on time.

I stood at the front of the sidewalk platform as I waited for the train to stop. This was the same platform my mother stood on when she planned to end her life in May 1993. How much had changed since then.

Although it was just another day as I headed into Chicago to teach at Moody Bible Institute, it seemed like only yesterday that I'd come home from prison. In March 2001, I had turned in my application to Moody—complete with references from a prison chaplain, a prison guard, and another inmate. That same day, my mother and I stayed on campus to attend president's chapel so we could hear Dr. Joe Stowell preach. We had already decided to introduce ourselves when he finished.

"I don't know if you remember me, but my husband and I met you at the Finishers Forum last year. I asked you if Moody accepts sinners." My mother smiled. "Well, here's that sinner."

Dr. Stowell did remember meeting my parents at the conference. My mother told him that I had been transferred to a halfway house and how well I had been adjusting to life outside prison. He graciously took down my name, and ever since he has been a friend and an encourager of this ministry God has put me in. After being officially released from the half-way house and federal custody in July 2001, I started as a part-time student at Moody. In the spring of 2002, I moved on campus as a full-time student.

Four years later I graduated with a bachelor's degree in Bible with an emphasis in music and biblical languages. I continued my studies in the biblical exegesis program, covering both Hebrew and Greek, at Wheaton College Graduate School as a recipient of the Charles W. Colson Scholarship for ex-offenders. It is the only scholarship of its kind.[23]

Although I never pursued it, God began to open doors for me to share my story of God's grace, both in my life and in the lives of my parents. When I got out of prison, friends of my parents asked me to share my testimony with their small groups and at men's breakfasts. Then more speaking engagements came along simply through word of mouth. Today, my speaking ministry has spread around the country and has reached four continents. It's funny to think back on Eddy Mendoza's crazy words when I was incarcerated in Brooklyn. I guess he was right!

Upon graduation from the Wheaton College Graduate School in 2007 with a master of arts, I knew that God had called me to the ministry of speaking on the issues of sexuality and HIV/AIDS. But on the days I wouldn't be speaking, I was open to more ministry opportunities to stay grounded in God's Word. So in God's sovereignty and the graciousness of the administration at Moody Bible Institute, I was asked to teach part-time as an adjunct instructor in the Bible department. Moody has been flexible with working around my speaking and traveling schedule. This will be my fourth year teaching Bible Introduction, and I absolutely love it. I have also just begun my first year of a doctorate of ministry program at Bethel Seminary in St. Paul, Minnesota, where I will focus my studies on sexuality and celibacy.

My parents were extremely supportive during my time at Moody and Wheaton, and they have been a great encouragement to me in my speaking ministry. But we knew that life on the road would be challenging.

Saddleback Church PICS

Here I am speaking at Saddleback Church's Global Summit on AIDS in 2007. I also spoke at the church's weekend services.

Long days of travel can be tiring, especially as HIV continues to weaken my body. So I asked my mother to be my travel and ministry partner. On the road, she helps me stay accountable and continues to cover me in prayer. Mom is and will always be my prayer warrior!

Not only does my mother travel with me, but I consider my parents to be partners in ministry. Several times, I have spoken together with my parents. We spoke at Willow Creek Community Church in 2006 and Saddleback Church in 2007, and God continues to open doors for me to speak at gatherings such as InterVarsity's Urbana and Moody pastors' and men's conferences.

God has sustained my health. Although I realize my physical limitations and I do tire out easily, I haven't started taking medications yet.[24]

I continue to see my doctor every three months for blood tests, and I attribute much of my health during the past thirteen years to eating right, sleeping well, exercise, and Chinese herbs. However, I will most likely begin taking medication soon, since the HIV continues to weaken my immune system. But again, my life is in the hands of the Father, and I know that every day is a gift—and that as a child of God, I must live each day with a sense of urgency.

This afternoon, I will be heading from Moody's campus to Wheaton College. I'm a part of the President's Task Force on Homosexuality, and we'll be meeting with the new college president, Dr. Philip Ryken. I've become quite involved at Wheaton College, also serving on their alumni board, the President's Task Force on AIDS, and the Colson Scholarship Advisory Committee. Then after a long day, I'll head home—to the home I came back to nine years ago.

It's hard for me to forget the day I returned home, with our front foyer covered with yellow ribbons. Each time I think about it, God's mercy washes over me, and I'm reminded of my parents' unconditional love for me. They will always stand at the door with arms wide open, ready to welcome me home, just like my heavenly Father. I know I can always, always come home.

Prayer, Redemption, and Holy Sexuality

An Eight-Session Guide to Out of a Far Country

For many, no biblical story is more powerful than that of the prodigal son (see Luke 15:11–32). The ungrateful younger son turns his back on his family while the older brother dutifully stays home. What's often missed in Jesus's parable is that the older brother also is a prodigal. Both of them need the father's love, just as each of us craves his waiting, open arms.

The story that is told in *Out of a Far Country* is a true account of God's seeking and saving two people who were lost (see Luke 19:10): a mother who was so distraught she had decided to kill herself, and a son whose pursuit of pleasure, money, and success led to arrest, prison, and a life-threatening illness. Both mother and son hit bottom, and at different times they both turned to God. The changes in their lives are nothing short of miraculous.

This discussion guide is designed to help you find lessons for your own life. We all have wandered, and every one of us wants to come back home. Whether you have been a prodigal son or daughter, or a prodigal parent, this guide will help you go deeper in your understanding of God's mercy, grace, love, and forgiveness. The eight-session study guide can be used in a variety of ways: when sharing with a friend over coffee or in a more formal group setting, such as a book-club discussion or small-group study. The questions are useful to anyone who is interested in knowing God more intimately as a loving Father.

Each week focuses on several chapters from the book. Feel free to highlight the topics and questions that speak most directly to your life. The questions are designed to encourage open discussion without putting anyone on the spot. The goal is to share with others as you deepen your relationship with God.

WEEK ONE

Read chapters 1 through 5 before the discussion.

1. At the beginning of Angela Yuan's story, she and Leon were struggling in their marriage. But when they first married, they were very much in love. In what areas of your life have you seen passion turn cold? Why do you think this happens in a marriage, a romantic relationship, a friendship, or in any relationship? (chapter 1)

2. After Leon and Angela found evidence of pornography in their son Christopher's room, they confronted him. But the conversation didn't go well. What was Angela's primary emotional response? Leon's? Christopher's? How would you have responded if you were the parent? if you were the son (or daughter)? (chapter 1)

3. Angela was in denial about Christopher's homosexuality before he officially came out to his parents. How was her refusal to acknowledge the truth unhealthy? What are some of the issues in your life that you are avoiding? How can we face the truth and refuse to live in denial? (chapter 1)

4. From Angela's perspective, her son rejected her. From Christopher's perspective, his mother kicked him out of the family. Both were hurt, and both felt they were the victim. This often happens

when both parties have completely different perspectives. Give an
example of how this has happened to you. What are some ways
we can do a better job of seeing another person's perspective?
(chapter 2)

5. When he was growing up, Christopher felt like an outcast. When
he was an adult and embraced by the gay community, he loved
the feeling of being completely accepted. The Christian community should be a place where anybody can come and feel accepted.
How can the church be more welcoming while holding fast to the
message of truth and redemption? How can you help your church
be more welcoming? (chapter 2)

6. Angela had a lonely childhood because her mother wasn't home
to care for her after school. As a result Angela promised herself
that she would provide a very different life for her family. What
are some positive experiences from childhood that you want to
replicate for your family, and which experiences do you want to
change? (chapter 3)

7. Just as Christopher was relishing the idea that he was free from
parental control and influence, his mother arrived to tell him that
she loved him—no matter what. Have you ever written someone
off only to have the person apologize and attempt to repair the
relationship? Is there someone in your life now with whom you
need to seek reconciliation? (chapter 4)

8. Christopher was desperate for relationships. In what ways are we
sometimes too desperate in pursuing relationships, to the point
that a relationship becomes an idol? How can we avoid this?
(chapter 4)

9. Angela decided she would stop allowing Christopher's dismis-
sive attitude to control her. How do we let other people—their
actions, their words, their attitudes—affect us? Can you give an
example? How did you overcome this (if it has been resolved)?
(chapter 5)

10. Angela was helped by reading a Christian pamphlet about homosexuality. When she called the phone number listed on the back,
a man from the ministry told her she couldn't change Christopher. She refused to accept what he said. How do you feel about
the man's statement and Angela's reaction? Can we change our
children? our spouses? If we can't change a person, what should
we do instead? (chapter 5)

11. As Angela was reading about shrikism, she was convicted of her
own self-righteousness. Have you ever tried hard to be right, even
at the expense of another person? Angela later realized that her
own sins were no less serious than Christopher's. If you have a
prodigal son or daughter, how do you compare your sins with
your child's? (chapter 5)

Week Two

Read chapters 6 through 9 before the discussion.

1. In hapter 6, Christopher told about someone who used criticism
and fear tactics to try to convince him he could change his sexual
identity. Why didn't this work? Have you ever dealt with a person
who tried to force you to change in order to meet his or her
expectations? (chapter 6)

2. When Angela returned home to Chicago, she feared she might
be going back to her old way of life and felt like giving up. When
you feel like giving up, what keeps you going? Give specific examples. (chapter 7)

3. Upon returning home, Angela set up a prayer closet where she
could spend quality time with God every morning. What daily
habits have you established or would you like to establish to
maintain a vibrant relationship with Christ? Is there a place
you have set aside as your place to pray and/or study the Bible?
(chapter 7)

4. In chapter 8, Christopher told about meeting a man named Kevin and the romance that developed. How do you feel about this story? If you desire to help a gay man or a lesbian find God, do you think your reaction to this story hurts or helps your mission? If you are gay or experience same-sex attractions and want to understand God's calling on your life, how does your reaction to this story help or hurt your pursuit of God? (chapter 8)

5. Kevin maintained that the Bible condemns homosexuality as sin and would refuse to discuss the issue while continuing his relationship with Christopher. In what areas do you tend to go against your inner convictions and refuse to follow God's truth? How do you rationalize ignoring biblical teachings in instances when obeying God would be difficult, awkward, or inconvenient? (chapter 8)

6. Angela characterized her marriage with these words: "Our unresolved issues seemed to define our life together." What unresolved issues define your life and relationships? How can you go about resolving them? (chapter 9)

7. As immigrants, Leon and Angela faced cultural differences and familial pressures that nearly drove them to divorce. What cultural or familial issues create strain in your life? What can you do to alleviate the pressures? (chapter 9)

8. Angela had no idea how her arguments with Leon affected Christopher—until she saw the drawing he made as a boy. How can you make your home a haven for members of your family, a place where they feel safe, loved, and treasured? (chapter 9)

9. Here is a trustworthy piece of advice for parents: the best gift you can give your children is to love their mother (or father)—and let your children see it. How can you love your spouse more completely, and how can you make it more apparent to your children? (chapter 9)

WEEK THREE

Read chapters 10 through 13 before the discussion.

1. Within just a few weeks, Christopher went from taking drugs to becoming a drug dealer. And while he sold drugs, he became a drug addict. Have you seen examples of sin quickly overtaking your life or another person's life? Explain. Why do you think Christopher was so susceptible to the entrapments of drugs and partying? (chapter 10)

2. Outside a huge circuit party (catering to gay men), Christopher encountered Christian protestors. The protestors believed they were upholding the truth; however, it was truth at the expense of compassion. How can Christians avoid damaging the message of truth by separating it from compassion, or conversely, muting God's truth in the name of compassion and love? (chapter 10)

3. The message proclaimed by the protestors was far from good news. Give examples of how Christians can proclaim the good news of the gospel by balancing truth with compassion. Can you think of someone who needs to hear you share God's good news? (chapter 10)

4. Christopher called his parents to tell them his school was planning to expel him. Angela and Leon had a difficult decision to make: should they "help" their son, or should they step back and trust the school administration to make the best decision? If they had intervened, they would have enabled their son. Enabling loved ones prevents them from facing the consequences of their choices, learning from their mistakes, and ultimately owning up to their problems. What are ways in which we enable those who are close to us? How can we prevent this from happening? (chapter 11)

5. Christopher was displeased when Angela told the dean of his school that a relationship with God took precedence over every-

thing else. Compare this example of speaking the truth (chapter 11) with the protestors outside the circuit party (in chapter 10). How are the two approaches different? Give examples from your own life that fit either situation. (chapter 11)

6. Christopher told the story of a porn star he befriended who ended up sick and alone in a public hospital in Chicago. Why do you think no one but the Yuans came to the hospital to visit this man? How did God use this situation in Christopher's life? What can you do to love those who are sick, alone, and in need? (chapter 12)

7. When Christopher found out that he may have been exposed to HIV, he was surprisingly calm and even resigned. Often people who live without Christ have the perception that we're just here to live and die, so we might as well live it up. Do you know people who live by this philosophy? What are some ways in which Christians can reach such people? (chapter 12)

8. Angela endured horrific childhood moments when she witnessed her mother having affairs in the bed where Angela slept. This secret shame continued to affect her until she was able to surrender those experiences to God. What tragedies or wounds from your past do you still hold on to? What keeps you from surrendering them? What tragedies or wounds have you been able to surrender to God? (chapter 13)

9. Angela's faith was so infectious that it helped bring her dad into a relationship with Jesus. Do you know people who have an infectious faith? What are some specific lessons we can learn from them? (chapter 13)

Week Four

Read chapters 14 through 17 before the discussion.

1. Christopher ran his drug-dealing enterprise as if it were a legitimate business, complete with office hours and financial records.

He seemed to be blind to the fact that it was wrong. How can people engage in wrongdoing and forget that their activities are not only illegal but also displeasing to God? (chapter 14)

2. Angela sent cards to Christopher, but he threw them away unopened. Even at that, Angela was planting seeds—Christopher knew that his mother hadn't given up on him. What are good ways to reach out to the people in our lives who seem unreachable? How can we persistently and repeatedly plant seeds in their lives? (chapter 14)

3. Angela faced heartbreaking disappointment when Christopher failed to show up at the airport for a Christmas visit. And she worried it would happen again when she and Leon traveled to Atlanta to visit him. How did Angela deal with that disappointment? How did Leon? How would you deal with a loved one's lack of consideration and open rejection? (chapter 15)

4. Christopher was good at ignoring his parents and starting arguments. If you had a rebellious son or daughter, how would you handle the situation? (chapter 15)

5. How did you react to the story about Christopher going into a restroom at church to take drugs? He had replaced worship of the true God with the worship of getting high. Can you relate to this? What thing (or things) in your life competes with your worship of God? (chapter 16)

6. Angela felt that Christopher was unreachable and completely hopeless. She and Leon didn't know how to deal with him. If they headed one direction, they would travel down the road of despair. If they headed the other direction, it would be toward hope. Have you ever found yourself at such a crossroads? How did you move forward? (chapter 17)

7. Angela sometimes wrote out her prayers, then prayed those prayers consistently over the years. Write out a prayer to God.

Be real, honest, and transparent. Now start praying this prayer and make it a part of your daily routine. Also, share the prayer with someone else—a prayer partner, a mentor, or the members of your study group. (chapter 17)

8. Angela wanted nothing more than to know that Christopher had received Christ. Parents often devote much of their prayer time to their children's education, career, health, and so forth. However, less time is spent praying for our children's relationship with Christ. Even in conversation, little time is spent talking about spiritual things while much more time is spent talking about school, work, friends, and family. Will you commit to spending more time in prayer for your children's spiritual welfare? Will you commit to talking to your children more about God? (chapter 17)

WEEK FIVE

Read chapters 18 through 21 before the discussion.

1. Christopher's addiction got worse and worse. How did you feel when Christopher's friend was shooting up? Do you agree that we all have a tendency toward addiction in some fashion, whether big or small? What addiction(s) have you overcome or are you overcoming? What helped you in overcoming addiction? (chapter 18)

2. After Christopher's apartment was raided by the police, he knew he was being monitored. But even that did little to change his habits. Instead of giving up drugs, he resorted to cheating on his urinalysis tests. Have you or someone you know ever been tempted to do the wrong thing, even when knowing there was a good chance of getting caught? How can one resist the impulse and do the right thing? (chapter 18)

3. Angela repeatedly prayed to God, "Do whatever it takes," so that her son would come to know Christ. Are you willing for God to "do whatever it takes" in your own life and in the lives of your loved ones? Why or why not? (chapter 19)

4. Angela began a list of blessings—even when her circumstances looked bleak. Begin writing a list of how God has blessed you—regardless of whether you're having a good day or not. Share some of the blessings with a friend or family member or those in your group. Try to make this a part of your daily routine. (chapter 19)

5. When Christopher woke up in jail, he thought he was living a nightmare. But he began to find hope when he discovered a Bible in a trash can. When have you felt that your life was a waking nightmare? Where did you find hope to continue in your journey? Share with the group what was most effective in giving you hope. (chapter 20)

6. Angela, who had never visited a jail before, was nervous on the day she first went to see Christopher. But she relied on God's promise from Isaiah 41:10: "Do not fear, for I am with you." When has God been there for you when you were unsure of the next step to take? (chapter 21)

7. Christopher's relationship with his mother was strained to the breaking point, but when Angela visited him in prison she broke through the tension. She even asked if she could pray with him, not being sure what his reaction might be. Have you ever stepped out in faith like this? Has anyone extended this kind of grace toward you? What happened as a result? (chapter 21)

8. Has God been hinting that you should reach out to someone? Who is it, and what does God want you to do for him or her? Try to reach out this week through a text message, an e-mail, a phone call, or a personal visit. Share your plans with the group. Next week, share the outcome. (chapter 21)

Week Six

Read chapters 22 through 25 before the discussion.

1. Discuss the moment Christopher received an HIV-positive diagnosis. Did you understand his emotional response in chapter 12, when he found out Derek was infected? Did his attitude change when he found out for sure that he was HIV positive? (chapters 12 and 22)

2. How did you respond when you read that Christopher was HIV positive? How would you respond if your best friend told you that he or she tested positive? How do you feel about hugging or sharing a meal with a person who has HIV? What can you do to help your church prepare to welcome people who have HIV? (chapter 22)

3. Angela said of Christopher's HIV status, "This worst nightmare was now a reality." What is your worst nightmare, and are you ready to face it should it become a reality? What are you doing to prepare for the storms of life? (chapter 23)

4. Christopher's experience in prison ranged from humiliating strip searches and mind-numbing stretches of hurry up and wait, to agonizing loneliness and the rare moment of inspiration and clarity. How has this book changed your perspective on the United States prison system? (chapter 24)

5. Angela used to think prisoners were monsters, but after her son was in prison, she began to see them as human beings. What assumptions do you make about inmates? What prejudices do you have about them, and how could you become more familiar with that segment of the population? What are the best ways for us to become aware of our hidden prejudices? (chapter 25)

6. When visiting Christopher in prison for the first time, Angela confessed that she hadn't been a perfect mother. She then asked

Christopher to tell her any weaknesses he saw in her. Have you ever asked anyone for constructive criticism? Do you think you are good at accepting constructive criticism? What are ways in which you can make yourself more open to such input? (chapter 25)

7. Christopher said, "I would have liked it if you had listened more to my heart than to my words." Often our rebellious children are really crying out for attention and love, but all we see are anger, rejection, and a bad attitude. What are some ways you can learn to listen to their hearts rather than their words? How can you ensure transparent communication to bring out issues that lie beneath the surface? What are ways in which we can express unconditional love but still hold to appropriate boundaries and consequences? (chapter 25)

8. Angela asked a judge to give Christopher "a sentence just long enough"—one that was long enough for God to change his life. What do you think about her approach? (chapter 25)

9. Jesus said, "I was in prison and you came to visit me" (Matthew 25:36). What does the Bible have to say about prisoners and the way Christians should respond to them (see Hebrews 13:3)? Do you know anybody in prison you could visit? Is there a jail or prison close to you where you could volunteer? What is holding you back? (chapter 25)

WEEK SEVEN

Read chapters 26 through 29 before the discussion.

1. Christopher said he and the other patients at the infectious-disease clinic tried to remain anonymous as they sat in the waiting room. What repercussions do you think could happen if their health status became public knowledge in prison? Do you think there are people in your church who are hiding something they

fear could be used against them? What can your church do to assure all people that they are safe to be open and transparent? (chapter 26)

2. Angela wasn't sure whether Christopher agreed to testify against an accused drug supplier in the hope his own sentence would be reduced or to follow God's will. Do you know someone (perhaps yourself) whose decisions are guided by self-interest rather than God's direction? Discuss. (chapter 27)

3. Eddy, an inmate in New York, encouraged Christopher to consider his calling to be a minister of the gospel. Have you ever identified a calling in someone else's life? If so, encourage that person to seek God's will this week. (chapter 28)

4. Have you ever felt a call from God? All believers are called to serve in some capacity right where they are. What has God directed you to do? How are you fulfilling that calling (or what is holding you back)? (chapter 28)

5. What do you think about Christopher's decision to testify against Abbas? Consider all the implications—personal safety, impact on his reputation, obedience to God's Word. Would you say he made a wise decision? What would you have done in the same situation? (chapter 28)

6. At his resentencing hearing, Christopher told his parents, "It doesn't matter where I am—whether in prison or out of prison—I'm going to serve the Lord." Do you have the attitude that you'll serve the Lord no matter what your circumstances? Or do you tend to say, "As soon as I get established, raise my kids, pay off my debts, and so on, *then* I'll be able to serve God"? (chapter 29)

7. Do you think Angela dealt with issues of shame as a parent because Christopher was in jail? When children go astray, do you think the parents should be considered responsible for their children's actions? Why or why not? If you have a prodigal, do you

experience shame? Although parents are responsible for the upbringing of their children, even a perfect parent can have rebellious children (God with Adam and Eve, for example). Are you
ready to release that guilt? Why or why not? (chapter 29)

WEEK EIGHT

Read chapter 30 through the epilogue before the discussion.

1. Christopher said he finally realized that "home" for him was in
   Chicago with his parents. Where is home for you? Is that where
   your home ought to be? (chapter 30)
2. Christopher defined an idol as "the one thing I think I can't live
   without." Have you ever asked yourself, *What do I think I can't
   live without?* Think through this question and conduct a personal moral inventory. Share the outcome with the group, or
   share something in the past from which you have been set free.
   (chapter 30)
3. A chaplain in the prison system told Christopher that the Bible
   supports homosexual relationships, but through Christopher's
   own reading of Scripture, he came to the opposite conclusion.
   Put in the broader context of sex, in what situation alone does
   God allow sex? Is this requirement gender specific? Use verses
   to back it up. (chapter 30)
4. Explain your understanding of Christopher's concept of holy
   sexuality—as opposed to heterosexuality—which is God's desire
   for all his followers. Do you believe God has created all people
   to be heterosexual, or is the concept of holy sexuality acceptable
   to God? Keep in mind that heterosexuality broadly includes
   sins such as adultery and lust, that Jesus was never married, and
   that according to Matthew 22:30, there will be no marriage in
   heaven. (chapter 30)

5. Is it too much to ask someone to be celibate—whether for a period of time or for life? What if you were called to celibacy, would you be able to embrace it? Why or why not? Do you celebrate your single friends' singleness or try to push them into marriage? (chapter 30)

6. Christopher wrote, "Change is not the absence of struggles; change is the freedom to choose holiness in the midst of our struggles." Is your goal simply to avoid doing certain things (vice, addiction, sin), or is your goal holiness? What are your thoughts on this? (chapter 30)

7. Christopher realized that the Bible never calls gay men and lesbians "abominations." However, God doesn't condone gay sex. How do you view gays and lesbians? Do you bristle when you think about this issue, or does your heart break for these people? Discuss. (chapter 30)

8. Christopher realized that his identity needed to be in Christ and not in his feelings, his struggles, or his sexuality. What have you based your identity on? Are you satisfied to live as a Christian and to be known as such, or do you feel the need to add other permanent identifiers? (chapter 30)

9. Christopher returned home and was overwhelmed with emotions as he saw more than a hundred yellow ribbons. Is there someone you need to welcome home? Or do you need to communicate to an estranged friend, spouse, or child that he or she is welcome to come home? Will you do something about that today? (chapter 32)

10. Look back through the book and consider the many moments that mirror Jesus's parable of the prodigal son. Examples include Christopher's leaving his family to live on his own in Louisville, Christopher's partying in Atlanta and around the country at circuit parties, Angela's waiting with open arms at the airport but

Christopher's not being on the plane, Angela and Leon's having the coat ready for Christopher when he was released from prison. What others can you think of?

11. As you've finished this book, has anything changed regarding how you feel or think about homosexuality, people with homosexual feelings, or the gay and lesbian community? What is your perception of addicts or criminals now? What did you learn, or how did your perspective change, as a result of reading this book?

NOTES

1. Colin Cook, *Homosexuality: An Open Door?* (Boise, ID: Pacific Press, 1985).
2. See Romans 8:39.
3. *Shrikism* is a word that is used in John and Paula Sandford, *Healing the Wounded Spirit* (Tulsa, OK: Victory, 1985), 241–70.
4. The motto of the United States Marine Corps is *Semper Fidelis,* "Always Faithful." Marines hold that even after they complete their active service and return to civilian life, they will always be marines: "Once a marine, always a marine."
5. Lamentations 3:22–23
6. Paul Jabara and Paul Shaffer, "It's Raining Men," recorded 1982 on *Success* by the Weather Girls, Columbia Records.
7. Christopher was accepted into dental school without receiving his bachelor's degree.
8. Psalm 46:10
9. An educational institution that receives funding under a program administered by the U.S. Department of Education is prohibited by the Family Educational Rights and Privacy Act (FERPA) from disclosing or discussing details of an adult student's education records with anyone but the student, unless the student waives his or her privacy rights by giving the educational institution written authorization and granting permission to do so.
10. See Isaiah 55:8.
11. See Galatians 5:22.
12. See 1 Corinthians 13:7 (NASB).
13. Don Moen, "God Will Make a Way," recorded 2003 on *God Will Make a Way: The Best of Don Moen,* Integrity Hosanna! Music/Epic/Sony, compact disc. Originally released in 1999.

14. Johnson Oatman Jr., "Count Your Blessings," 1897, public domain.

15. Helen H. Lemmel, "Turn Your Eyes Upon Jesus," 1922, public domain.

16. Horatio Spafford, "It Is Well with My Soul," 1873, public domain.

17. Psalm 56:8 (NASB)

18. Christopher mentioned in a previous chapter that the two worst kinds of people in the prison social structure were snitches and child molesters. This meant that when he was transferred back to the Federal Medical Center in Lexington, Kentucky, he worried that inmates would hassle him about testifying against Kareem Abbas. It turned out that a former friend and inmate was telling others that Christopher was a snitch. But fortunately, Christopher wasn't hassled much because he kept to himself. Plus, Christopher's friends were churchgoers, and they didn't care. Looking back, Christopher saw that God really did protect him.

19. See Leviticus 11:44–45 (NASB) and 1 Peter 1:16 (NASB).

20. For more on this idea, see Barry Danylak, *A Biblical Theology of Singleness* (Cambridge, UK: Grove Books, 2007), 19.

21. Luke 15:22

22. Irwin Levine and L. Russell Brown, "Tie a Yellow Ribbon Round the Old Oak Tree," recorded 1973 by Dawn featuring Tony Orlando, Bell Records.

23. For more information regarding the Charles W. Colson Scholarship for ex-offenders to attend Wheaton College, visit www.bgcprison ministries.com/index.php?id=83.

24. HIV medication is called ARV (antiretroviral drugs). The treatment also is called HAART (highly active antiretroviral therapy). Once a person begins taking these medications, he or she cannot stop. There often are side effects, but fortunately the newer medications have fewer of them and they are less severe.

CHRISTOPHERYUAN

UNDESERVING OF HIS GRACE · WWW.CHRISTOPHERYUAN.COM

More info at

www.christopheryuan.com

Video • Events • FAQs

Email

info@christopheryuan.com

Facebook

www.facebook.com/christopheryuan

Twitter

www.twitter.com/christopheryuan